ASHES FOR BREAKFAST

ASHES FOR BREAKFAST

SELECTED POEMS

DURS GRÜNBEIN

TRANSLATED BY

MICHAEL HOFMANN

FARRAR, STRAUS AND GIROUX NEW YORK

FARRAR, STRAUS AND GIROUX
19 Union Square West, New York 10003

Copyright © 2005 by Durs Grünbein
Translation and preface copyright © 2005 by Michael Hofmann
All rights reserved
Distributed in Canada by Douglas & McIntyre Ltd.
Printed in the United States of America
FIRST EDITION, 2005

Grauzone morgens (1988), *Schädelbasislektion* (1991), *Falten und Fallen* (1994),
Nach den Satiren (1999), and *Erklärte Nacht* (2002) were originally published by
Suhrkamp Verlag, Germany.

Some of these poems previously appeared, in slightly different form, in *Grand Street*,
The Literary Review, *London Review of Books*, *The New Republic*, and *The Times
Literary Supplement*.

Excerpts from "May 24, 1980" and "San Pietro" from *Collected Poems in English*
by Joseph Brodsky. Copyright © 2000 by the Estate of Joseph Brodsky.
Reprinted by permission of Farrar, Straus and Giroux, LLC.

Library of Congress Cataloging-in-Publication Data
Grünbein, Durs.
    [Poems. English & German. Selections]
    Ashes for breakfast : selected poems / Durs Grünbein ; translated by
Michael Hofmann.— 1st ed.
        p. cm.
    English and German.
    ISBN-13: 978-0-374-26074-3
    ISBN-10: 0-374-26074-5 (alk. paper)
    1. Grünbein, Durs—Translations into English. I. Hofmann, Michael, 1957
Aug. 25– II. Title.

PT2667.R842A24 2005
831'.914—dc22

                                                                2004053245

Designed by Gretchen Achilles

www.fsgbooks.com

1   3   5   7   9   10   8   6   4   2

CONTENTS

from SCHÄDELBASISLEKTION (1991)
Skull Base Lesson

from FALTEN UND FALLEN (1994)
Folds and Traps

from ERKLÄRTE NACHT (2002)
Configured Night

For upwards of twenty-five years, you have written English poems, and translated not poetry, but German prose. You felt no particular disquiet at this separation of powers. But finally, you don't want to spend your entire life in avoidance of something, in fear or disdain, however well grounded. There are translations of foreign poets to which you feel deep gratitude: Cavafy, Akhmatova, Zagajewski, Montale. You love your Waley and your Pound. In fact, the first poet you ever read, at the age of eight, was in translation: Zbigniew Herbert. (The poem was "From Antiquity," the one about the barbarians and the little salt god, and you've never forgotten it.) Above all, you feel an attachment to the idea that you have some German poet twin—the one who, unlike you, stayed at home—whom it is your duty and your sacred pleasure to translate into English.

I would never claim Durs Grünbein as my twin—he's a much better poet, and he's five years younger—but I did experience this feeling of kinship when I first met him and heard him read, ten or twelve years ago in Rotterdam, and many times since. For various practical, urgent occasions, I have supplied English cribs for his poems: another time in Rotterdam, once in London, at a talk in Hamburg. We share a derisive melancholia, an interest in amplitude (much more developed, in his case), a love of the Russian poet Joseph Brodsky, a fascination and a belief in the classics (again, much more developed in his case). At the same time, I am painfully aware of many things that divide us; medicine, neuroscience, animals, ancient history, contemporary art, responsible metaphysics are all avocations of Grünbein's of which I am, as they say in German, *unbeleckt*. Innocent. There is a formidableness, a dauntingness about Grünbein that I don't have, perhaps can't do, and find it difficult even to respond to.

You see, the different countries and different languages have evolved different types of poets—although, thrillingly, probably for the first time in history, one's formation as a poet is almost bound to be cosmopolitan nowadays and polyglot, and if it isn't, it damned well should be. I'm saying that I grew up as an English poet: small-scale, occasional, personal, wincingly witty, articulate about dirt. Grünbein is much more like another English poet, whom Brodsky also revered, but who was so much a one-off in or from the English tradition, that he described himself as "a minor Atlantic Goethe": W. H. Auden. Grünbein is squarely in the line of German poets: a *poeta doctus* and an intellectual. Further, there is a frontality and an abundance in him—massive poems, great sequences of numbered parts—that I can only wonder at. He has solved the problem of inspiration that Rilke worked at in his *Neue Gedichte* of 1907 and 1908. Grünbein has such facility and industry, it is as though there had been a Rodin in *his* life once as well.

What you translate has to come out of you; you have to be able to encompass it, in other words. You can't quite say things you couldn't have said, even if you have been given them to say. (In an odd way, this is more of a problem for poet-translators, who tend to suffer from self-consciousness and squeamishness, and a firmer sense of their own edges, than others, who are perhaps better able to slip into costume and lose their inhibitions.) You have to work on your own plausibility, your range, your idiom, your connections, and you try of course to extend them. Perhaps you're like a parrot, saying back things the way you've heard them said. (But always it has to come from you.) Temerity takes you further. And for me that's a real motivation: I should like to learn temerity. But there are many poems and places where Grünbein is too skillful, too euphoric, and too rhetorical for me to follow him. Sonnet sequences, poems praising Italy, his more neutral and classical—unPoundian—vein of classicism (what I think of in him as "marble"), anywhere, in fact, where rhyme—to Rilke the vector of praise—presents itself as an issue.

Accordingly, inevitably, I have to diminish him. Sometimes this will express itself in the range of poems that I feel able to tackle at all, sometimes in my inability to match, even to gesture at, his forms. (Though Brecht said: "When poems are translated into another language, most of the damage tends to be due to people trying to translate too much. Maybe they should confine themselves to translating the poet's ideas and attitudes.") Translation is most often described—perhaps can only be described—in metaphors, many of them drawn from the world of performance. (We've already had the actor, and the parrot.) Here, I'm tempted to say that translation is like tracing. Going over an original on onionskin paper. Well, in the case of those designs of Grünbein that most resemble architectural drawings—and there are many poems of his like that—I can't cope with the finickiness and the perfection. But what I suppose I do have—and Grünbein has declared himself willing to accept this, in fact, in his generosity, not even to see it as a *pisaller*, a second-best—is my own "line." My own idiosyncrasy and distinctiveness. I have the ability, I think, to go over lines, and make it seem like freehand. (I have learned to do this, both from my own writing and from making so many prose translations. The worst thing in a translation, it seems to me, is the appearance of being remote-controlled, *ferngesteuert*.) You have to look comfortable, voluntary. The Grünbein translations will look like—I hope to God they do look like—not the product of steel rulers and midnight oil, but like poems that want to be poems. I may not be able to limn them from the outside, but I hope I can animate them from within.

I am aware of course of the likelihood of there being something specious and sentimental about this argument. (I *would* say that, wouldn't I? Well, of course!) Actually, I'm not at all convinced that this is the better way, or that the specter of the point-for-point and formal translator—Lowell called him the "taxidermist"—has been put to flight. Auden, by way of a germane instance, used to say he first looked at the "contraption" of a poem, and only then at whatever it might express. I fear my versions of Grünbein won't be all that interesting as "contraptions." The exemptions I can see (once again, like Montale to Lowell) are those poems of his with bulk and quiddity, those poems of his that are interesting as prose.

I have perhaps one last thing to cheer me up and lead me on. As I've said, one of the things that Grünbein and I share is a love of the poet Joseph Brodsky. Really from the moment I first heard Brodsky, in 1981 as a recent ex-undergraduate in Cambridge, I had the sense of his poems existing in a weirdly trefoil or trinitarian fashion: there were the trim, carved stanza shapes, the vast oceanic surge and melody of them (especially of the Russian), and the wry modern first-person concreteness of them. And while I liked very much Anthony Hecht's "Lullaby of Cape Cod," and the poet's own astonishing English versions of "A Part of Speech," my favorite translations are a couple that were done by a Slavist, Barry Rubin, which are unrhymed and unscanned. Here is the beginning of "San Pietro":

> Three weeks now and the fog still clings to the white
> bell tower of this dull brown quarter
> stuck in a deaf-and-dumb corner
> of the northern Adriatic. Electric
> lights go on burning in the tavern at noon.
> Deep-fried yellow tints the pavement
> flagstone. Cars at a standstill
> fade out of view without starting their engines.
> And the end of a sign's not quite legible. Now
> it isn't dampness that seeps through the ocher and terra-cotta
> but terra-cotta and ocher that seep through the dampness.

What commends this to me is that it has so much of the "feel" of Brodsky, what I thought of as the third member of his personal trinity. The tired, almost baffled sentences, worn down to nerve and frazzled bone. Interest, personality, plight, speed of thought: are these not enough—more than enough—to furnish forth a poem, even if the original does have rhymes and bells and whistles? So, I thought, if I could get Grünbein to sound comparably dense and inhabited in English, I would be doing all right by him. Tickling his nostrils with the smoke of a satisfactory olfactory sacrifice.

As I say, Grünbein works in big poems and sequences, but it was not always thus. There are little Polaroids from his young years in Dresden, under the old management. The poet himself may be a little uneasy about these now, but his translator admires some of them very much for their unhindered voice, sprayed out across a page: big vocabulary, correct syntax, and still a sense of something being blurted. The mood of nauseated contempt in, say "All About You," is admirable, and bound to appeal to the author, himself, once, of a volume, called *Acrimony*. A few phrases: "*einer immerfort gestrigen Politik,*" "an insistently ancestral politics"; "*zwischen Kinderwagen und Scharen räudiger Tauben, die einen Wirbel machen beim Futtern,*" "between the baby carriages and the flock of mangy pigeons that fly up in a sort of haute volée gobbling"; "*das übliche Kino des Status Quo Minus,*" "the usual BBBBBB films"; "*schlenderst du einfach ein wenig weiter zur nächsten Kreuzung, sehr langsam,*" "but instead you just gander on very slowly to the next crossing." There are differences—inevitably, there are differences—but I like to think what I offer is harmonious and possible, with its bird words and assonances. As I say, what I'm anxious *not* to do is offer something exotic, wooden, pointless, and dead.

That poem came out of the mid-eighties, "from the Eastern part of my life," as Grünbein inscribed my copy. Then, there is a thirty-nine-part sequence called "Variations on No Theme" (the title is pure Brodsky, the switch of geography likewise!) from the early nineties. "*Variationen auf kein Thema*" is Grünbein's "A Part of Speech," thirteen-line sections, attractively set in and out, little essays, memories, a lexicon of modern life, autobiography in a solvent of metaphysics, *Betrachtungen.* I've had a go at the whole thing, all thirty-nine steps, but I couldn't pretend to you that they're all equally good or equally finished. In fact, the question of "finish" in poetry translation is what *macht mir zu schaffen*—does my head in, I would say in English. In fiction it's easy. I put the original away, and fiddle with the English to the point where I start to undo my corrections and put back things I had before. Then it's done. But what to do with a poem? If I "take it away," and work at it in the same way, until every line has just enough material and just enough music and just enough interest, then surely it would become one of my own poems. And it might be a long way from the original. Is the secret, then, merely to reduce its exposure to me, "undercooking" it, as it were? Possibly—but that's precisely my objection to a lot of poetry translations, that they are undercooked. They might be glimmerings and beginnings of poems, but full of clumsinesses and dullnesses; no English poet would dream of offering something so "half-baked," so *halbgar,* so intermittent. But it has to be in some more verifiable relation to the original. It doesn't merely face the reader; Janus-faced, it has to be looking back over its shoulder at the German, too. It's a real problem, and I don't know what the answer is. Lowell, whom my editor encouraged me to imitate, wrote in his introduction to *Imitations*: "I have tried to write live English and to do what my authors might have done if they were writing their poems now and in America," and: "I have been almost as free as the authors themselves in finding ways to make them ring right for me." But then the poets Lowell translated were, with one or two exceptions, not his living contemporaries, and he was not offering the first or principal way into their work for an English readership. There may be a little security to be had from printing the facing German texts, but that always cuts both ways, I feel, as a reader. You can't settle to anything; the original faces down the translation. Also, German comes a long way below French, Spanish, Italian, on the list of feasible foreign languages, and only just above Russian, I think, in my more pessimistic moments. Anyway, on to a couple of sections of "Variations on No Theme." First an early memory, the infant Grünbein:

> What a bloody little leprechaun you once were,
>   A wrinkled imp with knotted
> Arms and legs. Bluish skin,
>   As though kicking for your life,
> Early concerned with your impending death.
>   And it all began so unconsolably,
> With a piercing yell, when the world
>   Moved into your lungs with a rattle.
> With a shock ("so much light!"), a slicing
>   Of deft scissors and knives
> Into the only flesh that wasn't you.
>   The umbilicus was like the thread,
> The Fates' love of sundering from the get-go.

I'm uneasy about my repeating "with" in a slightly different sense in lines 7 and 9, and I'm very pleased with the sudden shift of idiom, "love of sundering from the get-go," but other than that I have nothing much to confess to, here.

The situation is very different with the other "Variation":

> Back in front of the telephone, under the cheese cloche,
>   The cosh, the Alexander Graham Bell jar,
> No sooner was the door shut, you froze, a cynosure,
>   A dead ringer for passersby on the sidewalk,
> Staring at the dial-pad, digits
>   Like the stellar magic forest
> In the night sky . . . decimal mandala
>   Tempting you by its availability
> Sudden nearness, whispers, betrayal,
>   Egad, love, even—all of it seemingly
> Hardwired, a sort of "I'll call you" life.
>   The numbers no sooner punched
> Than a voice explodes in your brain.

If the previous "Variation" was dutiful, this one is wildly interesting! It begins with the very first words, "Back in front," and carries on through little rappish rhymes and raffish portmanteaux ("cosh" and "cloche"; "the Alexander Graham Bell jar"), through extravagant diction ("cynosure") and puns ("a dead ringer"), the bizarre ejaculation "egad," and a further pun in "punched" at the end (although the very best thing, for my money, is the phrase about the "'I'll call you' life"). It is in an interesting relation to the German. I don't know why this happened like that to this poem. Perhaps it was the single-sentence rush of the thing; perhaps it began with the cheese cloche, and turned, as is in the nature of cheese, into a nightmare.

Another thing Lowell says in his introduction to *Imitations*—which seems to have become a sort of half-controversial Bible to me!—is this:

> Boris Pasternak has said that the usual reliable translator gets the
> literal meaning but misses the tone, and that in poetry tone is of

course everything. I have been reckless with literal meaning, and laboured hard to get the tone. Most often this has been *a* tone, for *the* tone is something that will always more or less escape transference to another language and cultural moment. I have tried to write live English, etc. etc.

This, like a lot of Lowell's critical prose, is strangely self-annulling—the tone, everything to get the tone, then (of course) not the tone, but, hey!, some other tone!—but I still think there's a germ of truth and interest and encouragement here. I'm thinking of one of the newest of Grünbein's poems that I've tackled—which, nevertheless, dates from the previous millennium: in addition to my other difficulties and humiliations, Grünbein writes new poems rather faster than I can get around to translating his old ones!—a brisk and typically stylized "autobiography" called "Vita Brevis." Once again, Brodsky is a sort of godfather here, he *steht Pate* to the translation: as before with "A Part of Speech," now with a fortieth birthday poem called "24th May 1980." Both "Vita Brevis" and "24th May" have a kind of adventurous swagger about them. I love the long lines with the big caesuras:

I saw the zero beribboned, and the colossus ground down by dwarves.
The born deserter: sooner die than take aim at the heart.
I puked out of tanks, cried myself to sleep in barracks.
Shaved my skewed grin over a bucket, under canvas.
I did in my knee at soccer, but my soul fared much worse.

By way of comparison, here is a bit of Brodsky, so you might see where I—and perhaps Grünbein, too, for that matter—came by some of that sound:

From the height of a glacier I beheld half a world, the earthly
width. Twice have drowned, thrice let knives rake my nitty-gritty.
Quit the country that bore and nursed me
Those who forgot me would make a city.
I have waded the steppes that saw yelling Huns in saddles,

worn the clothes nowadays back in fashion in every quarter,

planted rye, tarred the roofs of pigsties and stables,

guzzled everything save dry water.

Otherwise, just a couple of observations on the beginning and end. "In a rotten nutshell" isn't as compressed as *"Kurz und bös,"* but it tries to atone by at least containing two words or allusions to *Hamlet*, which I hope have some bearing on the speaker of the poem, and the GDR: the thing about "something rotten in the state of Denmark" (Paul Celan used wonderfully to speak of "something rotten in the state of the D-mark"!), and living in a nutshell, "and count myself king of infinite space." Likewise, I can't come up with end rhymes like Hawaii and *dawai*—the poem is in rhymed quatrains, *abab*—but by way of compensation I offer the power and pith of English vernacular speech: "something exotic *before you hand in / Your dinner pail.* What say the Hawaiian beaches?"

Here, anyway, is the history of my apprehension, and then of my *bruk zagoghaft* little shoots of translation. *Honi soit.* Finally I had the feeling I've come so far, I can't now turn back, which, as Kafka said, is the point that must be reached.

MICHAEL HOFMANN

London, June 2004

GRAUZONE
MORGENS

(1988)

EINE EINZIGE SILBERNE BÜCHSE

Sardinen plattgewalzt
zwischen den Gleisen &
an den Seiten quillt

überall Sauce raus rot
wie Propangasflaschen
                    (& ziemlich

bedeutungsarm) sie allein
unter sovielem Strandgut
im Landesinneren hält schon

was dieser Morgen an Schönheit verspricht.

A SINGLE TIN

of sardines flattened
between the tracks &
the orange sauce

squeezed out the sides
the color of propane bottles
                (& pretty

lacking in significance) alone
among so much flotsam & jetsam
so far inland keeps

whatever this morning promises
        by way of beauty.

An manchen Tagen wußten wir einfach
    nichts Bessres zu sagen als
        ›Gleich passierts‹ oder ›Geht
      schon in Ordnung . . . ‹ gelangweilt in

überheizten Bibliotheken wo unsere Blicke
    bevor sie glasig wurden wie
        Rauchringe schwebten
      unter den hohen Kassettendecken
        alexandrinischer Lesesäle. Die
      meisten von uns

    wollten fort (nach New York oder
        sonstwohin): Studenten mit

komisch flatternden Stimmen
    gescheiterte Pläne umkreisend immer im
        Aufwind und manche vor

    melancholischer Anarchie süchtig
      nach neuen Totems, Idolen
        gestriger Revolutionen und dem
        zum x-ten Mal
akupunktierten Leib der Magie. Man kam
    ziemlich billig wenn man den ganzen Tag
      dort verbrachte (besonders
    im Winter) zwischen den
        kurzen Pausen allein

There were days it was all we could manage
        to say, "It may never happen" or
                "Something will turn up . . ." bored in

overheated libraries where, in moments
        before they completely glazed over
            our glances found themselves drifting
              like smoke rings
            under the lofty coffered ceilings
              of Alexandrian reading rooms.
            Most of us

    wanted to get away (to New York
        or someplace): we were students

with funny cracked voices
        enthusiastically turning
            failed projects in our heads, and some of us

              in our melancholy anarchy
                    fell thrall to new totems, idols
      of gone revolutions and the
multiply acupunctured body of magic.
      If you spent the whole day there
        (especially in winter),
            it was pretty cheap, alone
              between the short intervals

mit seinen postlagernden Sorgen miets-
schuldig, die Stille wie
Nervengas aus den Büchern
saugend all dieser
sanften Bestien (. . .) und manchmal
gab es selbst dort im Einerlei
dieses Treibhausklimas ein wenig
lebendige Überraschung—
(Trilce, César!). Ich

erinnere noch genau eines Nachmittags
im Sommer das
raschelnde Zwielicht als ich
beim Scheißen aus einer Nebenzelle der
Bibliothekstoilette
gedämpftes Atmen und Stoß auf Stoß
schnell sich steigern hörte: mein Herz
flog plötzlich auf und ich
erschrak wie ein ganzer
Schmeißfliegenschwarm vor dem

Liebesspiel zweier Männer die stumm
aneinander arbeiteten
schwitzend und selbst-
vergessen wie fremde
kentaurenartige Wesen auf einer

überbelichteten Fotografie.
Schwer zu vergessen mit welcher
Erleichterung sie nachher
frischgekämmt jeder
hochrot und mit cremigem Teint

with our poste restante worries, owing
for the rent, sucking the silence
out of books like nerve gas
from all these mild beasts (. . .) and sometimes
even in the unvarying
hothouse climate there was a
somewhat living surprise
(Trilce, César!). I

remember one particular
summer afternoon
the rustling dusk
I was in the toilet taking a dump
when I heard rapid breathing
from another cubicle and an accelerating thumping
and I was alarmed as an entire
swarm of blowflies at the

love of two men silently belaboring
one another
sweating and oblivious like strange
centaurlike creatures on an

overexposed photograph.
Hard to forget
the relief with which,
with fresh combed hair
red faces and creamy complexions

einzeln an mir vorübergingen und nur
ein Augenzwinkern (durch mich
hindurch) verriet mir:
Sie hatten sich kennengelernt.

they separately walked past me and only
a wink (a wink that went
through me) assured me:
they had gotten acquainted.

Reglos für Augenblicke ähneln sie
    Spinnen von fern wie sie an
speichelsilbrigen Fäden hängen oder

Matrosen in blitzender Takelage vor
    Hochhausfenstern, die das Licht
gegenüberliegender Hochhausfenster spiegeln,

Fassadenkletterer in derselben nervösen
    Schwingungsstille wie das
                    kaum merkliche
          Flimmern der Iris beim Aufblick.

Später sieht man aus Stahlseilen
                feingeknüpft ihre Kokons
   hoch über Straßenschluchten gehängt,
            die gespenstischen Schaukeln.

Kein Wunder, daß sie so leicht sind.
    Was für seltsame Lebewesen
          in diesem kalten Monat November.

Motionless for moments at a time,
    they resemble distant spiders, the way they
hang on silver saliva threads, or sailors

on glittering rigging, in front of the windows
    of office blocks reflecting the light
from the windows of office blocks opposite

climbing in the same taut
    suspension as the
        barely perceptible
        flicker of the iris as you look up.

Afterward you see their cocoons
    woven from steel wire
    dangling high over the crevasse of the street,
        the ghostly swings.

No wonder they're so light.
    Strange unseasonable creatures
        in the November chill.

Dieses Staunen wie hell selbst die
    abgeschiedensten Vorstadtwege
in einer Neuschneenacht liegen —
        da war sie wieder
die Untrüglichkeit der Haikus.

Oder ein andermal Meister Bashô als dieser
    bleiern sich windende Fluß
        die Elbe

Kloake mit ihren wenigen quellebendigen

Wirbeln längst ölgeworden doch
    eines Morgens wieder entufert lag —
Diese Freude der Überschwemmung! Diese

plötzlich so unscheinbar eingebetteten
    Brücken! Es war als irrten
die Landungspontons strudelnd in Seenot
        Möwenspähtrupps zogen
an weichen Vorgebirgsrändern vorbei und die

Regenfluten brachten das Einerlei des
    verdammten Elbtalkessels zum
Brodeln. Nicht wahr: eine seltene Suppe.

Denk nicht ich sei gehässig Bashô. In mir
    ist nicht einmal was übrig blieb
von ›alten Soldatenträumen‹ kein ›Sommergras‹ —

Astonishment at the brightness
       of even the remotest back alleys
on a night of fresh snow—
         there it was again
that haiku-unerringness.

Or on another occasion Master Bashō
       when this leadenly coiled river
               the Elbe

open sewer with its few animated

tourbillons long since turned to oil one
       morning lay there without its banks—
flooded with joy! Those

suddenly improbably low-slung
       bridges! It was as though a few
pontoons were adrift Mayday Mayday
          squadrons of gulls
drifted past the gentle slopes and the

torrential rain brought the whole mélange
       of the dammed up Elbe valley
to the boil. Some soup.

Don't think me malicious, Bashō. In me
       there isn't even what was left over
from "old soldiers' dreams," the "summer grass"—

lauthals zu sein: ich habe es satt so ganz
    gramgesättigt zu leben von einem
undurchdringlichen Augenblick an den

nächsten gespannt in einer Stadt alternd
    in notgedrungenem Schweigen in dieser
Talversunkenheit schwerer Kuppeln und

schmaler durchbrochener Türme — Dresden
    grausam zurückgebombt um ein
weiteres kaltes Jahrhundert der Müdigkeit
    und betriebsamen Enge die Straßen
        voll Echos verhohlener Echos.

(Wie das den Tag füllt: die alten
    Alarmrituale von Straßenbahnen und
Mittagssirenen der ganze Lärm der abends
    längst aufgelöst ist in ein
beliebiges Nichts.) Denn so regelmäßig

arbeiten der Kühlschrank mein Herz und
        am Fenster
magisch die beinereibende Fliege daß es
    fast scheint alles sei jetzt im
Einklang Matsuo — irgendein zen-

buddhistischer Witz und die letzten
    Redensarten ringsum wie
        Speisereste verteilt.

to be mouthy: I'm fed up
        with being so grief-stricken pinned
from one impenetrable instant

to the next in an aging city
        in enforced silence in this
valley depression of heavy domes and

narrow needle-spires—Dresden
        viciously fire-bombed back
another cold century of tiredness
        and narrow bustle the streets
                full of echoes of secret echoes.

(How it fills the day: the old
        alarm rituals of streetcars and
noonday sirens all the noise that by
        evening is dissolved into
random nothing.) Because

the refrigerator my heart
        and the magically leg-rubbing fly
                  by the window
are all so assiduous that it
        almost appears as though there were a
harmony of everything Matsuo—some Zen

Buddhist joke and a few congealed
        phrases served
            like leftovers.

Undurchdringliche Augenblicke eng
   aneinandergereiht wie
Gerüchte im Schein einer immerfort
        gestrigen Politik, eine

Folge schnell wechselnder Grau-
     samkeiten, das
         Nonsens-Ping-Pong-
   Geschwätz einiger Zeitungs-
leser auf einer Parkbank und du
       wie du die Windstille

genießt unter niedrigem Himmel (im
   Schauspielhaus gegenüber proben sie
     Shakespeare . . . ›Wir Hu-
manisten . . .‹).
      Du wartest und
    beugst dich vor zwischen
       Kinderwagen und
   Scharen räudiger Tauben die

einen Wirbel machen beim Füttern —
     Du siehst ihre Köpfe ab-
    getrennt
      blutig im Rinnstein, ein
   schillernder Tagtraum, ringsum

bespritzte Statisten in einem
     Attentatsfilm (Der
Mord an Leo Trotzki) oder das übliche

A series of impenetrable instants
      jammed up together like
rumors by the light of an insistently
                ancestral politics, a

sequence of rapidly changing grue-
          somenesses, the moronic ping-pong
              chatter of a few newspaper
readers on a park bench, and you
          you're just enjoying the calm

under a low sky
      (in the theatre opposite they're rehearsing
         Shakespeare . . . "We
humanists . . .").
             You wait and then
         you choose your moment between
              the baby carriages
         and the flock of mangy pigeons that

fly up in a sort of *haute volée* gobbling—
              You can picture them
              with sev-
       ered
        bloody heads in the gutter, a
    vivid daydream,

           the bespattered extras in an
             assassination flick (*The
Murder of Leo Trotsky*) or the usual

Kino des Status Quo
>Minus . . . , aber dann
>>schlenderst du einfach
>ein wenig weiter zur
>>nächsten Kreuzung sehr
>>>langsam, denn
dieser Tag gehört dir.

BBBBBB films . . . but instead you just
                  gander on very slowly
         to the next crossing, because
today is all about you.

Prenzlauer Berg sonntags die dunstige
Schwüle in den von
Autos verstopften Straßen. Ein Junge
in Jeans

streichelt ein Mädchen lässig beim
Telefonieren am Apparat dicht
vor der Hauswand zersplittertes Glas. Sagt
›Nichts los heut‹ und wendet

sich um in die Richtung aus der
der Schrei eines
verunglückten Kindes kommt aus-

gestreckt wenige Meter vor dem
zerquetschten Ball.

Prenzlauer Berg of a Sunday sultry
               haze of traffic-
choked streets. A boy in jeans

strokes his girl calmly while
               talking in a call box
broken glass just in front of the entry. Says,
                   "Oh, nothing," and turns

to face
               the screams of a child

lying a few feet away from its equally
               flattened ball.

Soviele Tage in denen nichts sich
    ereignete, nichts als die
knappen Manöver des Winters, ein paar

Schneehügel morgens, am Abend längst
    weggetaut und der seltsame
Augenblick im Kasernenviertel war

ein exotisches Flugblatt: als dieser
    kleine Soldatentrupp Russen in
grünem Filzzeug schweigend ein

Zeitungsbündel bewachte und ich las
    ›КОММУНИСТ‹ obenauf und
es fiel mir die Zeile ein ›Denk

an die Uhr am Handgelenk
                Jackson Pollocks.‹

So many days and nothing
     happening, only
sketchy winter maneuvers

a couple of snow heaps in the morning
     melted away by evening, and the strange
moment in the barracks

was an exotic cameo: when that
     little troop of Russians in
green felt uniforms silently

mounted guard over a stack of
     newspapers, and I read "КОММУНИСТ" on top,
and the line came into my head: "think of

the wristwatch on Jackson Pollock's wrist."

Da war diese grüne Hülle der Zahlungs-
        fähigkeit, ein Gefühl kurze Zeit
                oben zu sein . . . schnell verwelkt.

Und irgendwer hat dir ein Fliegenpapier
        an den Rücken geheftet, du
ahnst es schon (›incommunicado‹).

Müde Heimkehr nach einem Abend voller
        Geschwätz delirierender kleiner
            Sorgen fast ohne
                Anstrengung. Verflucht

bist du klebrig Süßer, am ganzen
        Körper, die Poren mit un-
            scharfen Linsen von Schweiß

ausgefüllt. ›Viertel nach 2 . . . ‹, und ›Kein
            Traum in Aussicht . . . ‹ , nur
diese ziellose Müdigkeit. In New York

        hättest du todsicher jetzt den
Fernseher angestellt, dich zurückgelehnt
                blinzelnd
vom Guten-Morgen-Flimmern belebt.

There was this green carapace of bank-
            ability or do I mean creditworthiness, a feeling of being
                  briefly on top . . . soon gone.

And someone gummed a piece of fly-
            paper to your back, you could feel it said
something like "incommunicado."

Exhausted return home at the end of an evening
            full of talk of delirious little
                  anxieties with next to no pain.
                        Sweetheart,

you're damned sticky, it's all over you
            the pores gummed up with out-of-focus
                  lenses of sweat.

"Quarter past two . . ." and "no
            dream in prospect . . ." just
                  this directionless tiredness. Whereas

            if you'd been in New York, you know,
you'd just have turned on
                        the TV,
and blinking settled blinking back,
            animated by the early early show.

Was für liebliche klare Objekte doch
        Badewannen sind makellos
                emailliert ganz unnahbar mit dem

heroischen Schwung rundum gußeiserner
        Alter Ladies nach ihren
                Wechseljahren noch immer frisch.

Typische Immobilien (wann hätte jemals
        sich eine von ihrem Fleck
                gerührt) sind sie doch immer

wieder von neuem gefüllt, aller Dreck
        aufgelöst in die Kanalisation
                fortgespült muß unfehlbar

durch dieses enge Abflußloch auf dem
        Wannengrund. Wahre Selbst-
                mordmaschinen auf ihren

stummeligen Beinen, Warmwasserbetten mit
        Platz genug für ein ein-
                zelnes vögelndes Paar in

sovielen Wohnungen etwas wie eine Oase
        voller nostalgischen
                Schaums.

What adorable objects bathtubs are, enameled
    and sleek and altogether
        unapproachable with their

heroic curves of wrought-iron
    old ladies still frisky
        after the menopause.

Typical chattels (when did
    one of these ever get up
        and go) and nevertheless

continually replenished, all the dirt
    dissolved and swilled
        into the sewage system

is forced through that narrow
    stopper hole in the base. Real sui-
    cide machines on their

stumpy legs, warm-water-beds
    with just enough room for a sing-
    le copulating couple

in so many apartments, something like
    an oasis of nostalgic
        bubbles.

Ein neues Gedicht hat
begonnen an diesem
Nebelmorgen von Garcia
Lorcas Ermordungstag. Eis
essende Kinder und alte
Männer mit komisch
geschwollenen Köpfen
begegnen uns auf der
Straße zum Standesamt wo

unser Kreuzschiff vom
Stapel gelassen wird ohne
das übliche Winken ganz
und gar ungeweiht aber
dennoch von allen bösen
Familiengeistern besetzt.

Wir hatten das Schweigen
gelernt mühlos vorm
Abend wie eine dunkle
Sehne zu spannen: man
sah uns nicht an wie
uns zumute war beim
Verlöschen der Ziele.
Westwärts zog ein Paar
kleiner Wolken, die
Stadt färbte den Himmel
über sich grau und
ich sagte, es hätte mir
Freude gemacht über
Müllhalden mit dir zu
schlendern. Du aber

UNTITLED

A new poem began
on this foggy morning
of the anniversary of García
Lorca's murder. Children
eating ices and old
men with strangely swollen
faces passed us on our
way to the registry office

where our cruise ship
was launched without any
of the usual waving and cheering
unblessed but for all that
still crewed by the evil
spirits of both families.

We had learned to span
silence quite effortlessly
in the evening like a taut
sinew: they couldn't see
what we felt like
as the targets were wiped.
Two small clouds
moved off in a westerly direction,
the city dyed the heavens
gray overhead and
I said I had enjoyed
wandering over the garbage
heaps with you. But you

trugst die verrückten
Schuhe: knallgelb und
wir hatten es eilig als
ein besonders kühler
Nieselregen begann.

were wearing those crazy
shoes: canary yellow, and
we were in a hurry as
a particularly cool drizzle
started to fall.

Alles fängt an kompliziert
       zu werden
             wenn dir das
Elefantengrau dieser Vor-
       stadtmauern den
             letzten Nerv
raubt für die Unmengen
       freundlicher Augenblicke.
Dann geht plötzlich alles
       schief
             du bist nur noch
aufgelegt zu geduldigen
       Elegien
             montierst lustlos
ein bißchen an diesen
       verbogenen Mobiles aus
               Tele-
graphendrähten und altem
       Gitterwerk —
             traurig traurig:
nichts will mehr fliegen
       nichts sich bewegen lassen
von einem leichten Wind.
       Natürlich ist alles dann
nur noch ein Rinnsal
       vor-
       gestriger Freuden
             du läufst
steif wie der
          BRUDER DES
       BLUTEGELS durch diese
langweiligen Straßen

Everything starts getting
        a wee bit complicated
                when the elephantine
gray of these
        outlying suburbs
                takes away the last
of your tolerance
        for so much
                friendliness.
Then everything goes a-
        gley
                and the most
you can handle is patient
        elegies
                unenthusiastic tink-
ering
        with those skewed
                mo-
biles of phone wire
        and old fencing
                sad sad:
nothing will fly nothing stir
                in the torpid air.
Of course, everything's
        just a trickle
of the day before
                        yes-
                terday's pleasures
                        you prowl through
the boring streets
        stiff as the
                leech's

weichst
Mülltonnen und Stapeln von
Bierkästen aus und vor all
diesen Abrißhäusern und
öden Garagenhöfen
Plakatschwarten an Litfaß-
säulen und
Schrebergärten
peinlich umzäunt bist du
die meiste Zeit
nichts als
ein drahtiger kleiner Statist
hin- und herbugsiert in den
Staffagen eines schäbigen
Vorstadtkinos
4 Jahrzehnte
nach diesem Krieg.
Klar daß
fast jedes Gedicht dir
vor Müdigkeit schlaff wie
ein loses Spruchband zum
Hals heraushängt:
dieser Vers
so gut wie ein anderer
hier
auf einer Grautonskala . . . Es gibt
keine Wölfe mehr nachts und
Asasels rauhes Gebell ist
das Taxihupen am Morgen. Der
Frühling ist dieser Urin-
gestank altersschwacher
Maschinensäle und

little brother step
           around
                    garbage cans and pallets
of beer crates
           past so many
                    condemned tenements
garages yards
           placards swelling on
                    public
noticeboards
           and pedantically fenced in
                    allotments
you're nothing but a
           wiry little extra
                    most of the time
pushed back and forth
           in the frames of
                    a grotty suburban flick
4 decades
           after the war.
                    Stands to reason
almost any poem
           is going to make you puke
                    with boredom
like an ill-fitting
           speech bubble:
                    one line's
                             as good as another
on this graygray color chart . . . There are
                    no more wolves at night and
Asasel's rough bark is
                    the honking of taxis in the morning.
Spring is the pissy smell
                    of incontinent metallurgy

                    Herbst der
            Asphaltglanz auf Dächern und
Ästen ein Netz haarfeiner
                Risse zurückgelassen vom
Ascheregen quer über den
                    dreckigen Spiegelungen
des Lärms (d. h. natürlich nur
                wenn du dich mies fühlst).
                            Ansonsten
geht wohl auch das.

and fall

    the asphalt gleam of roofs

and tree branches a web of

        delicate cracks left from the

rain of ashes

        all over the dirty reflections

of noise (of course, only if you're

        feeling really grungy).

          Otherwise

it's probably just about OK.

mit alten Autoreifen, Glas,
Sperrmüll und der Attrappe
eines kleinen Wehrs

aus Zellophan und Schrott,
in dem inmitten Schaums
auf einem Ölfilm ausgesetzt

ein grüner Badefisch sich
zwischen Zweigen schaukelnd
leicht um seine Achse dreht.

Kommt
Wellen klaren Wassers, kommt.

with old auto tires, broken glass,
household junk, and the bones
of a small fort

of polystyrene and crap,
where, on a lagoon of oil
with *cotorni* of bubbles

a yellow plastic duck
bobs round on its axis
caught by low-lying branches.

Come,
waves of crystal waters, come.

Sie fand sich in einem
        Straßenbahntraum
ohne Notbremse gefangen
        im trüben Licht
zwischen leeren Pilsner-
flaschen, Fetzen von
Packpapier, Kotzelachen

Konfetti und Plastik-
        sitzen zu öd
darauf Platz zu nehmen:

sie war eine Spanierin
        (schwarz von den
                Strümpfen bis zur

Mantilla). Barfuß und mit

umwickeltem Zopf à la
        Carmen wieder allein
                (Aschermittwoch).

Geschwängert vom üblen

Mundgeruch des Soldaten,
        dessen Ausgang ein
Reinfall war, stand sie
wie seekrank im letzten
        Wagen und es war

fraglich wie sie da
        wieder rauskam.

OLÉ

She found herself
    caught in a streetcar dream
without an emergency brake
      in the gloaming
among empty beer
  bottles shreds of packing-
paper, puddles of vomit

confetti and plastic
    seats too upsetting
to be sat on:

she was Spanish
  (all in black from her
        stockings to her

mantilla). Shoeless and with

her plait twisted round her head
    à la Carmen alone again
        (Ash Wednesday).

Impregnated by the foul

breath of a soldier,
    whose outing had
gone wrong, she stood
in the last carriage feeling
    seasick and you had to wonder

frankly how she would
      ever get out of there.

Wenn dir was läuft plötzlich
als Katastrophe erscheint

bleib nochmal leicht. Sag es so
daß man am andern Ende das

klare Gefühl einfach nicht
loswird: Genauso wie der

hätte man's auch gesagt.

Es gibt heiße Medien und es
gibt kalte Medien Gedichte

egal in welchen Brüchen auf
was für Zeug immer GEDRUCKT

bleiben kalt (und wenn sie
noch so heißgekocht sind).

Dabei liegt Heiß und Kalt
oftmals gar nicht sehr weit

auseinander und manchmal
schlägt eins ins andere um:

Aus dem fauligsten Pathos
wird das belebende Sprudeln

der Luftblasen aus einer
Seele auf Tauchstation. Denn

If what goes on suddenly
strikes you as atrocious

try and stay calm. Say it
in such a way the person at the other end

can't help thinking: I probably
wouldn't have put it any differently

myself.

There are hot forms and
cold forms and poems

no matter how you break them and
what you print them on

are always cold (no matter how
hot they were at the manufacturing stage).

And yet hot and cold
sometimes aren't even all that

far apart and it has been known
for the one to turn into the other:

the ripest pathos
becomes the animating gurgle

of air bubbles from a soul
in the depths. Because

was ist schon die Surrea-
listik der Ängste gegen die

maßlos zufälligen kleinen
Tricks eines Gedichts.

what is the whole surreal jokeshop
of terrors compared to the

infinitely chance little
tricks of a poem.

Zwischendurch gibt es dann
manchmal Tage an denen

habe ich wieder Lust ein
Gedicht anzufangen der Art

wie sie noch immer nicht
sehr beliebt sind. Ich meine

eins ohne alle meta-
physischen Raffinessen oder

was als Ersatz neuerdings
dafür gilt . . . diese Tour

zynisch abzuknien vor dem
Stelzengang der Geschichte

oder gebrochenen Blicks im
harten Ost-West-Marathon
wie nur je ein verdammter

Schatten Dantes von Seiten-
stechen zu klagen. Gedichte

sagte mir neulich jemand

reizten ihn nur wenn sie
voller Überraschungen sind

aufgeschrieben in diesen
seltsamen Augenblicken da

From time to time
I have these days when

I feel like embarking
on a poem again

of a kind that still isn't
all that popular. I mean

one without any meta-
physical refinements or

that thing that lately has stood in
for such . . . that type of

cynical genuflecting
at the stilted progress of history

or standing gasping akimbo
in the tough East-West marathon
as if you were one of

Alighieri's damned
with a stitch. Poems

someone said to me the other day

only attracted him if they
were full of surprises

written at those
odd times when

irgendetwas noch Ungewisses
ein Tagtraum eine einzelne

Zeile von neuem anfängt und

dich verführt.

something still inchoate
a daydream a single

line begins somewhere and

undoes you.

Du verfolgst deine eigen-
sinnigen Pläne du stellst

die Bilder um ordnest die
Augenblicke aber du hörst

ihnen nicht zu wie sie
ganz anders ordnend ihre

eigensinnigen Pläne ver-
folgen wie sie die Bilder

umstellen zufällige Gesten
zeigen in denselben Räumen

sich anders bewegen bemüht
dir nicht zuzuhören. Das

ist der springende Punkt.

You pursue your own
eccentric designs you re-

fine the images you order
the moments but you don't

listen to them
as quite differently in their own ways

they pursue their eccentric
designs refine

images show chance movements
move differently

in the same spaces and damned
if they're going to listen to you. That

is the nub.

Seltsam was mich noch immer
umhaut ist diese Plötz-

lichkeit mancher Augenblicke.
Z. B. das helle Blinken der

Bauchseite wenn ein Delphin
sich herumwirft und durch den

hochgehaltenen Reifen am Arm
der Dompteuse springt. Oder

der kalte Sekundenbruchteil

wenn eine 61er Bildröhre auf
einen Schlag implodiert und

dir erst über den Splittern
klarwird daß da immer schon

kein Gedächtnis war (was also
sollte verlöschen?). Vermutlich

kommt alles von dieser feind-
lichen Lichtung in deinen

Träumen dem schiefen Tableau
aller toten lebendigen Dinge

Strange what continually a-
mazes me is this suddenness

of some instants.
e.g., the bright flash

of a dolphin's belly
on its upside-down arc

through the hoop the swim-
suited assistant holds aloft. Or

the brittle split second

when a '61 cathode ray tube
implodes at a stroke and

it is only looking at the shards that it
dawns on you that there never was

any memory (so what was there
to be wiped?). Presumably

all that is generated from
the menacing clearing

in your dream the crooked
tableau all the dead living things

tagsüber abgedrängt in jene
diapositiven Regionen wo
jedes so unabänderlich wirkt

nicht wahr und trotz allem
kaum länger dauert als ein

paar tausend REM.

repressed by day into those
shady slide-show regions where
everything seems so immutable

—yes?—and for all that
lasts barely longer than

a couple of thousand REMs.

(LIED)

Sieh genau hin, ehe sie dich
    für blöd verkaufen.
        Amigo, die klarste

Einsicht liegt in der Luft.
    Du mußt nicht
schneller sein oder cleverer.
    (Das gehört hier dazu.)

Geschäftigsein macht sich
    bezahlt (und scheint besser
als Glücklichsein). In den
        Stunden der Unter-

haltung bleibt noch die
    raschelnde Zwietracht
        von Konkurrenten, das

Dickicht enttäuschter Blicke.

In toten Studios Tonband-
    zirpen zu den kopierten
        Gesten, ansonsten
        Gesichter wie auf —

geschlagene Zeitungen voller
    Kommuniqués und Sehn-

(SONG)

Take a good look, before they
      sell you a pup or down the river.
          Amigo, the clearest

insight is in the air.
        You don't need to
be quicker or cleverer.
      (That's part of it.)

There is gainful
      employment (which makes it prefer-
able to the pursuit of happiness). In the
        hours of enter-

tainment there is still
      the discord bridling
          between rivals, the

thicket of disappointed glances.

In dead studios, tape-
      twitterings to the synched
        movements, otherwise
      faces like o-

pen newspapers full of
      communiqués and the de-

sucht nach Televisionen am
    Abend und dem
        Betrug einer Hand

über den Körper gleitend
    wie über Metall.

sire for a little television
    at night and the
             deception of a hand

caressing your body-
    work.

Ende der Eiszeit . . . (ein Film?): Tschuang-tse
    trifft Ezra Pound im Hades
        und schlägt ein Kreuz über ihm.

Die Glücksgötter grinsen, die neuen Menschen
    blinzeln träg in die Sonne.
        Niemand mehr träumt den Traum

von einem Zeitalter, in dem die Maschinen
    Köpfe tragen an ihrem Platz
        zwischen Pflanze und Tier.
    . . . .

Im Handumdrehn aus dem Lärm einer Stadt
    fliegst du als Zeitpfeil
        durch den Science-fiction-Spiegel

hinaus in das galaktische Schweigen der
        Dichter des Tao.

End of the ice age . . . (a movie?): Chuang-Tsu

        meets Ezra Pound in the underworld

               and makes the sign of the cross over him.

The fortune gods grin, the new humans

        blink lazily in the sun.

            No one anymore dreams the dream

of an age in which machines

        with heads occupy the place

            between flora and fauna.

            . . . .

In the blink of an eye, you fly

        out of the noise of a city like time's arrow

            through the science-fiction mirror

out into the galactic silence of the Tao poets.

SCHÄDELBASISLEKTION

(1991)

Zum Andenken an I.P. Pawlow
Und alle Versuchshunde
Der Medizinischen Akademie der
Russischen Armee

PORTRAIT OF THE ARTIST AS A YOUNG BORDER DOG (NOT COLLIE)

To the memory of I. P. Pavlov
And all the laboratory dogs
Of the medical academy of the
Russian armed forces

Eingefrorener Hund
Wurde wiederbelebt.

›Das ist ja sonderbar!‹ schrie der
Mit der dünnen Stimme.

›Und er kommt nicht allein‹
Antwortete die Fremde.

(Fortsetzung folgt)

Frozen dog
Brought back to life.

"Astonishing!" called the man
With the reedy voice.

"And he's not the only one,"
replied the stranger.

(to be continued)

1

Hundsein ist ein leerer Parkplatz am Mittag.
›Nichts als Ärger . . . ‹ und Seekrankheit an Land.
Hundsein ist dies und das, Lernen aus Abfallhaufen,
Ein Knöchel als Mahlzeit, Orgasmen im Schlamm.
Hundsein ist was als nächstes geschieht, Zufall
Der einspringt für Langeweile und Nichtverstehen.
Hundsein ist Kampf mit dem stärkeren Gegner
Zeit, die dich schwachmacht mit rennenden Zäunen.
Sovieles an Vielzuvielem auf engstem Raum . . .
Hundsein ist diese Fahrt mit der Geisterbahn
Sprache, die trickreich den Weg verstellt,

Falle für Alles.

Hundsein ist Müssen, wenn du nicht willst, Wollen
Wenn du nicht kannst und immer schaut jemand zu.
Hundsein?

    Ist dieses Übelriechen aufs Wort.

1

Being a dog is an empty car park at noon.
"Nothing but trouble . . ." and seasickness on land.
Being a dog is this and that, taking instruction from garbage heaps,
A knuckle sandwich for dinner, mud orgasms.
Being a dog is whatever happens next, randomness
The mother of boredom and incomprehension.
Being a dog is being up against a bigger opponent
Time, which does you in with endless chain-links.
So much of too-much in a tiny space . . .
Being a dog is a ride on the ghost train of language,
Which keeps throwing clever obstructions your way.
Being a dog is having to when you don't want to, wanting to
When you can't, and always somebody watching.
Being a dog?
          It's the bad smell attaching to your words.

2

›Geh aus dem Licht‹ sagst du und meinst im Glas
Des Spiegels, blind vom Hinsehn, diesen Dämon
Der dich (Quecksilberblick!) bejahrt bejaht.
Mit hartem Strahl durchdringt er dein Gesicht
Wie ein Spion vom Clan der Röntgengeister.
Wenn du dich wendest, wendet in dir Angst
Vorm Unumkehrbarsein zur Flucht nach vorn.
Bis etwas feststeht . . .

                 hinter den Grimassen.
Noch im Phantombild wirst du, beim Gehirntest
Sofort erkannt. Wenn auch nur halb und halb.
Ein Andrer in den andern gehst du fremd
Wie sie in dir fremdgehn.

                 Die Stirn vermauert
Ist jede Zuflucht schnell durcheilt. Zu spät
Kommt alles erst ans Licht durch Autopsie?

2

"Get out of the light," you say, talking to the demon
In the glass gone blind with looking,
Giving you the glad eye these many years.
Its harsh glance pierces your face
Like a spy from the clan of the X-ray spirits.
When you turn your back, your fear of
Going rigid turns with you.
Till something's certain . . .

                         behind the grins.
Even in your phantom image, the brain scan
Picks you out. If only partially.
An alien among aliens, you stand out
As they stand out in you.

                     With walled up frontal bone
Every refuge is left behind you. Will it be too late
By the time the autopsy sheds its bit of light?

3

. . . zig Jahre Dienst mit Blick auf Stacheldraht
Landauf landab im Trott hält nur ein Hund aus,
Der was ihn gängelt anstaunt, früh schon brav.
Im Schlaf noch wird ihm jedes Loch im Grenzzaun
Heimtückisch klein zum Einschuß hinterm Ohr.
Ein sattes Schmatzen zeigt: Auch Hunde träumen.
Was ihm den Maulkorb feucht macht, ist der Wahn
Daß Parallelen irgendwann sich schneiden
Wo Pawlow für den Rest an Psyche steht
(Instinkt, mobilgemacht, ein Zickzack-Kompaß)
Ist Dialektik nichts als . . . Hundetreue;
Sinn für die Stimmung in *his master's voice.*
So kommt es, daß er erst im Abgang klarsieht,
Am Ende des Prozesses.
                    ›Wie ein Hund.‹

3

. . . umpteen years of service with a view of barbed wire fence,
Trotting back and forth upcountry and down, only a dog could endure,
Captivated by his lead, trained to behave from infancy.
Even asleep, the tiny gap in the wire
Shrinks to the size of a bullet hole behind his ear.
A smacking of the lips proves even dogs have dreams.
The thing that sets his juices flowing is the idea
That parallel lines meet somewhere.
Where Pavlov stands for the residue of spirit
(instinct mobilized, a zigzag compass)
Dialectics is nothing but . . . dumb loyalty;
An ear for the feeling in his master's voice.
The moment of clarity is the lightening before death,
At the end of the trial.

"Like a dog."

4

Alt siehst du aus, young dog. Atomzeitalt.
Neugierig morgens, schwer von Rest-Rationen
Bildsatter Träume streunst du in den Tag,
Gebremst vom Autostrom im Smog, den Sprachen
Gedruckt auf breitgewalztem Holz, dem Brei
An dem nicht zu ersticken es viel List braucht.
Denn was du sein sollst, gibt dein Phänotyp
Der Fetisch, jedem sichtbar, vor: ein Deutscher.
Weiß . . . männlich . . . mittelgroß . . . brünett.
           Das reicht
Vielleicht für siebzig Jahre *Kampf ums Dasein.*
Wenn's hochkommt, hält Geduld den Rotz zurück.
Doch droht mit Schlimmsten immerhin auch dir
Die Dummheit,
      das Gesumm der Hirnmaschine
Von der es heißt, sie produziert sich selbst.

4

You look old, young hound. Atom age old.
Curious in the mornings, heavy with leftover scraps
Of vivid dreams, you amble into your day,
Penned in by the traffic streaming by, the lingo
Printed on flattened wood pulp, the mush
It takes plenty of cunning not to gag on.
Because what you are supposed to be, your phenotype
The fetish, broadcasts to everyone: a German.
White . . . male . . . medium build . . . brown hair.
                                         It might do
For seventy years of existential struggle.
At best, patience might hold back the drool.
But the greatest threat, even to you,
Is from stupidity,
                     the buzz of brain activity,
Of which it's said, it creates itself.

5

Aus dem verramschten Rausch der frühen Jahre
Geführt aufs Glatteis scheuer Sachlichkeit
Frierst du am Nullpunkt ein vor Zeichenstarre.
Durch dich hindurch geht was Versprechen spricht,
Ein Schwindsuchtsog, der Wort, Blick, Geste leert.
Die grellen Träume bleichen aus beim Waschen
Chemisch entfärbt, mit blödem Zeug bedruckt.
Die Resistenz am Ende des Jahrhunderts
Zieht sich geheimnislos ins Hirn zurück.
Was jetzt noch wachhält, Schwachkopf, ist Gelächter
Über ein Tier, tief in sich selbst verstrickt.
Sonst gibt es nichts, was ernst zu nehmen wäre.
Gefragt, woran ich Tag und Nacht gedacht hab
Sag ich aus List vielleicht nochmal ›An nichts.‹

5

From the junked buzz of the early years,
Led out on to the black ice of shy objectivity,
You go rigid at zero with an excess of signifiers.
The roar of empty promises,
Vacuuming out words, gestures, expressions.
The garish dreams lighten in the laundry,
Chemically bleached, printed with some nonsense or other.
Resistance at the century's end retreats
Blatantly into the brain.
The only thing to keep you up, simpleton, is laughter
At an animal caught in its own toils.
It's the only thing you could begin to take seriously.
Asked what I've spent night and day thinking about,
I sometimes have the presence of mind to reply: "Nothing."

Der Mensch, nun ja . . . das alphabetisierte Tier,
Das einzige das lügt, gehorcht der Logik
Von Augenmaß und Täuschung. Was das heißt
Siehst du beim ersten Blick in eine Zeitung.
Beim zweiten . . . Vorsicht . . . bist du schon dabei.
Was hilft dir Skepsis, seit soviel geglaubt wird
Daß du wie Stickstoff Illusionen atmest
Die als Gerücht längst reiner Traumstoff sind.
Statist des Alltags mit dem Kopf im Nebel
Denk an Sokrates.
                    Wenn der schwor ›Beim Hund!‹
Fiel eine Welt aus Meinungen in Scherben.
Wie jedes Kind schon weiß, echt paradox
Bringt gleich das erste Wort ein Mißverständnis
Das nur durch Wiederholung sich vergißt.

6

Homo sap., the animal with letters after its name,
The only one to lie, to obey the logic
Of appearance and deception. As you'll see
If you cast your eye once over a newspaper.
Twice . . . careful now . . . and you're caught.
What good is your skepticism when so much is taken on trust.
When you breathe (like nitrogen) illusions
That are rumored to be the stuff of dreams.
Bit player, with your head in the fog,
Think of Socrates.
                    When he swore, "By my dog!"
A world of opinions smashed to smithereens.
As any child will tell you, the very first word
Paradoxically produces a misunderstanding
That it takes repetition to clear.

7

Glücklich in einem Niemandsland aus Sand
War ich ein Hund, in Grenzen wunschlos, stumm.
Von oben kam, was ich zum Glauben brauchte.
Gott war ein Flugzeug, wolkenweiß getarnt
Vom Feind, mich einzuschläfern, ferngesteuert.
Doch blieb ich stoisch, mein Revier im Blick.
Wenn ich auf allen Vieren Haltung annahm,
Zündstoff mein Fell, lud mich der Boden auf.
Im Westen, heißt es, geht der Hund dem Herrn
Voraus.
            Im Osten folgt er ihm — mit Abstand.
Was mich betrifft, ich war mein eigner Hund,
Gleich fern von Ost und West, im Todesstreifen.
Nur hier gelang mir manchmal dieser Sprung
Tief aus dem Zwielicht zwischen Hund und Wolf.

7

I was happy in a sandy no-man's-land, I didn't do verbals,
I was a dog, wanting for nothing or not much.
The faith I needed to live by came down from on high.
God was an airplane, camouflaged like a cloud
By the enemy, remote-controlled, to lull me to sleep.
But I remained stoical, eyeing my terrain.
When I stood to attention on all fours,
With my dynamited pelt, the ground earthed me.
In the West, so they said, the dog precedes
His master.
      In the East, he trails him—at a distance.
As for me, I was my own dog,
In the suicide strip, equidistant from East and West.
It was only here that I sometimes performed
My *salto mortale* in the gloaming between dog and wolf.

Verstand, wie *Joe* sagt, die Dreigroschen-Hölle
Ist dieser Ort, wo sich das Ich eins pfeift;
Wo sich auf Abstand halten Angst und Neugier.
Die Angst: es könnte bald an seinem Rand
Spurlos verschwinden auf dem Weg der Neugier.
Der Neugier: wie sich's lebt, befreit von Angst.
Daraus ergibt sich leicht ein kleines Drama
Entlang der Grenzen, vom Verstand markiert
Durch immer neues unverwandtes Streunen.
Ich bin nicht hier, sagt es.

                        Ich bin nicht dort.
Und sein Versteckspiel zeigt: Ich ist kein andrer
Als dieser Grenzhund, der sich selbst bewacht.
Wer garantiert dir, daß er dich nicht anspringt
Gesetzt, du ziehst dich still aus dem Verkehr?

8

Reason, as Joe says, this two-bit hell
Is this place where the self whistles up a storm;
Where fear and curiosity strike a balance.
Fear: lest it suddenly disappear
Without trace on the path of curiosity.
Curiosity: what it might be like, to live without fear.
It produces a little drama
Along the border marked by reason
Through perpetually new straying.
I am not here, it says.
                              I am not there.
And its games of hide and go seek confirm:
I is none other than this border dog
Keeping a watchful eye on itself.
Who will guarantee that it won't leap on you
If you quietly remove yourself from circulation?

Hört euch das an: Ich sei so sanft gewesen
Daß man mich nun als Haustier halten will,
Heißt es in einem Nachruf noch zu Lebzeit.
Mir wird ganz schlecht, wenn ich sie flöten höre
Von handzahm, kinderlieb und treu. Geschwätz!
Für alles Fremde findet sich ein Kennwort.
Sieht aus, als sei ich nun von Zeit ereilt
Und meine Stimme schwimmt im Eingeständnis:
›Halb war ich Zombie, halb enfant perdu . . . ‹
Vielleicht hat mich da draußen irgendwann
Der Raum verschluckt, wo sich der Sichtkreis schließt.
Von nun an soll mein Double für mich sorgen.
Mein Trotz wird ausgekotzt mitsamt der Frage:
Ob Haustierhirne schließlich leichter sind?

9

Now listen to this: in the obituary they wrote about me
In my lifetime, they said I was so sweet-natured
That they wanted to keep me as a pet.
It makes me ill to hear them drooling
About my loyalty, my affection, my trustworthiness around children.
Tripe! There's a term for everything alien.
Looks as though time has caught up with me,
And my voice is swimming in the confession:
"I was half zombie, half *enfant perdu* . . ."
Perhaps eventually space gulped me down
Where the horizon closes up.
My double can look after me from here on in.
My orneriness is puked out, plus the question:
Do pets have lighter brains?

10

Wie gut nur, daß man meiner Stirn von außen
Den Film nicht ansieht, der im Innern läuft.
›Mein Leben rückwärts . . . ‹ oder wie ich blindlings
Im Sperrgebiet durch die verminten Zonen strich,
Selbst nur ein Strich in einer offnen Gleichung.
Nun ist sie nicht mehr offen, ich bin frei.
Die Landschaft sinkt zurück, ein neuer Baugrund.
Seit ich hier raus bin, kennt mich niemand mehr.
Der Sand löscht aus.

     Wachtürme sind vergeßlich
Wie Augen, von den Höhlen abgelöst.
Die zwei, drei Namen für den Ort der Trennung
Sind schon verblaßt.

     Nichts mehr verrät den Trick
Durch den ein Streifen Land zum Zeitloch wurde.
Wie gut nur, daß man meiner Stirn nichts ansieht.

10

Just as well you can't read my thoughts,
The film I've got running in my imagination.
"My life in reverse . . ." or how I blindly
Patrolled the minefields in no-man's-land,
Myself just a cipher in a simultaneous equation.
No longer simultaneous, and I'm free.
The landscape sinks back, a new brownfield site.
Ever since I got out of here, no one knows me anymore.
The sand blots.
        Guard towers are forgetful
As eyes, relieved by sockets.
The two or three names for the place of separation
Are already gone.
        Now nothing is left to recall the trick
By which a strip of land became a hole in time.
Just as well you can't read my thoughts.

11

Und du? Hast du vergessen, wo du herkommst?
Wird dir nun klar, wie groß der Schaden ist
Sovieler Jahre Peinlichkeit und Komik . . . ?
Was für ein Land, in dem ein Wort zum Tag
Viel mehr erregt als das noch nie Gesagte,
Das somit ungesagt bleibt.
                                            Wessen Stimme
Verschluckt sich beim Versuch den Fraß zu kauen?
Sogleich zu wissen, was geschieht, was nicht
Kann Raffinesse sein.
                                            Hier war es Lethargie
Wie kopflos strammzustehn vor Müdigkeit.
Was heißt schon Leben? Für alles gibt's Ersatz
Wo nur Hypnose herrscht und ›Dienst ist Dienst‹.
Mach dir nichts vor, im Paradies der Hunde
Ist Pisse an den Bäumen Stoff zum Träumen.

And you? Have you forgotten where you're from?
Is it starting to dawn on you how much damage was done
By so many years of humiliation and slapstick?
What a country, where a word on something topical
Provokes more than the unsayable
Remaining unsaid!
                              Whose voice
Is swallowed during the attempt to chew your gubbins?
To cotton on right away to what's happening, and what isn't
Can be sophistication.
                              In this instance, it was lethargy
That prompted you to stand to attention brain-dead with exhaustion.
What is life anyway? Everything's replaceable
Where hypnosis rules and *my duty right or wrong.*
Don't kid yourself, in the paradise of dogs
Piss on a tree trunk is the stuff of dreams.

Hund unter Hunden nachts im Schußfeld wach:
  Wie war das noch, der Bauch gibt acht? Worauf?
  Daß du gepreßten Kuchen frißt in Preußen?
Was war es, das dir in den Rücken trat,
War es die Großhirnrinde, die da sprach
  ›Ich weiß‹? War es die Zufuhr frischen Bluts?
Was für ein Hundeleben und um welchen Preis.
  Daß du ein Opfer bist, was soll der Quatsch?

Nur Ethologen haben den Komplizenblick
  Der Angst begreift. In ihren Studien kommt
  Das Tier als Mensch oft vor. Was mich betraf
Ich lag in einem langen Schlaf. Ich war
Ein Automat, der leicht auf Knopfdruck kam.
  Wohin ich kam, kam ich umhin. Von A
Nach B (und umgekehrt) der schnellste Weg
  Wo Mißtraun Bögen schlägt, ist die Ellipse.

Reiß dir kein Bein aus . . . Künstliche Intelligenz
  Hat für den Fall der Störung vorgesorgt.
  Schon in der Frage, wer dich repariert
Falls die Mechanik streikt, steckt der Defekt.
Als *L'homme machine* . . . von La Mettrie in Schutz
  Genommen brauchst du keine Alibis
Du funktionierst, das reicht. Und good old Hobbes
  Kommt für den Schaden auf im Dienst der Ordnung.

Niemand kann sagen, was ihm fehlt eh nicht
  Der Schock ihm hilft. Aus Ignoranz gestürzt
  Fliegt dir dein ganzes Leben auf. Im freien Fall

Dog among dogs awake at night in the firing zone:
> How was it again, your stomach growled? What at?

> At the biscuits they tossed you in Prussia?

What was it that kicked you in the back,

Was it the cerebral cortex that said, "I know"?

> Was it the supply of fresh blood?

What a dog's life, and at what a price.

> No underdog-victim twaddle, please.

It takes ethnographers, with their coconspirators' look,
> To understand fear. Animals often appear as humans

> In their works. As far as I'm concerned,

I was embarked on a long sleep. I was a machine

That liked it when my buttons were pushed.

> So and so many strikes per minute. I struck. They struck.

For the apprehensive, the quickest way from A to B

> (and back again) is the ellipse.

Break a leg . . . Artificial intelligence
> Has planned ahead in the event of a breakdown.

> The only question remaining is

Who will fix you if your machinery breaks.

As an *homme machine*, you enjoy La Mettrie's

> Protection, and don't need an alibi.

You function, that's enough.

> And good old Hobbes will pay the bill.

Unless he's tried shock treatment, no one can say
> What he lacks. Plunged from ignorance,

> Your whole life opens up. In free fall,

Zieht ein Projektor die Verlust-Tabelle durch.

Lochstreifen nackter Angst. Vor meinen Augen Schwarz.

    Kann sein, es ist Verblendung, die mir sagt:

Nicht erst seit Vico oder Machiavelli sind

    I due occhi della storia blind.

A projector scans the table of defeats.
Punched strips of naked fear. Things go black
        Before your eyes. Could be dazzlement
That says it wasn't Vico or Machiavelli
        Who said history is blind in both eyes.

FALTEN UND FALLEN

(1994)

Fortfahren . . . wohin? Seit auch dies
   Nur der fällige Ausdruck
Für Flucht war, für Weitermachen
   Gedankenvoll oder -los.
Was aufs selbe hinausläuft, wie?
   Zug um Zug einer neuen
Erregung entgegen, einem Gesicht
   Zwischen den Zifferblättern
Im Schaufenster, Brillen für Liebe,
   Für schärferes Fernsehn, Särge
Und Möbel zum schnelleren Wohnen,
   Wo Engel an Kassen saßen, taub
Gegen ihr süßes, nekrophiles Hallo.

To digress . . . where to? Even that, remember,
    ("Goof off") was just the usual formula
For flight, for carrying on elsewhere
    Thoughtlessly or otherwise.
Comes to pretty much the same thing, no?
    Assembling a new excitement
Feature by feature, a face
    In among the clockfaces
In the window, the glasses for love,
    For higher definition TV, drive-through
Funerals and furniture for faster living,
    Angels manning the checkouts, deaf
To their sweet, necrophile, hel*lo*.

Wieder vorm Telephon, in der Vitrine
   Wie unterm Glassturz, kaum
War die Tür zu, erstarrt, ein Objekt
   Für Passanten am Straßenrand,
Starrst du auf dieses Tastenfeld, Ziffern
   Wie der stellare Zauberwald
Am Nachthimmel . . . dezimales Mandala
   Das mit Erreichbarkeit lockt,
Mit plötzlicher Nähe, Geflüster, Verrat,
   Sogar Liebe — alles codiert
Wie seit langem im voraus, ein Leben
   Auf Abruf, und kaum gewählt
Explodiert eine Stimme in deinem Kopf.

Back in front of the telephone, under the cheese cloche,
  The cosh, the Alexander Graham Bell jar,
No sooner was the door shut, you froze, a cynosure,
  A dead ringer for passersby on the sidewalk,
Staring at the dial-pad, digits
  Like the stellar magic forest
In the night sky . . . decimal mandala
  Tempting you by its availability
Sudden nearness, whispers, betrayal,
  Egad, love, even—all of it seemingly
Hardwired, a sort of "I'll call you" life.
  The numbers no sooner punched
Than a voice explodes in your brain.

Unterwegs zwischen Mutter und Äther
  Auf Sendersuche, den Pulsschlag
Des blutigen Hasen im Ohr, anästhesiert
  Wie unterm Handschuh die Haut
Von tausenden Innenstimmen, — wer weiß
  Wer da jedesmal sang, klanglos
Wie im genetischen Chor der Refrain.
  Großmutters *Ach* oder das *Hhm*
All der steinernen Gäste im Keller . . .
  Bis den Mauern der Schweiß
Ausbricht und du dich flüstern hörst:
  Was für ein Aufwand an Panik
Für ein wenig abgeleckt werden, nachts.

Traveling the dial between mother earth
　　And mother ether, the pulse beat
Of the bleeding rabbit in my ear, desensitized
　　Like the skin under a leather glove
By the thousands of inner voices—who knows
　　Whose the individual voice was,
Undetectable in the genetic choir.
　　Grandmother's *Ach* or the *Hhm*
Of all the stone guests in the basement . . .
　　Till the walls break out in sweat,
And you hear yourself whisper:
　　What a lot of panic
Just for a spot of suction, at night.

Und morgens schießt aus der Dusche . . .

    Wasser, was sonst? Rot und Blau

Steht auf den Hähnen für Heiß und Kalt.

    Daß die Haut sich in Streifen

Abschält, bleibt ein alberner Alptraum.

    Kein Dorn im Handtuch, kein Blut

An den Fliesen — das Röcheln im Ausguß

    Heißt Hygiene, nicht Tod.

Und ob Seife noch immer aus Knochen

    Gemacht wird, der Schaum

Auf den Handlinien trocknend, sagt nichts.

    Ängstlich belebt, an den Haaren

Herbeigezerrt, stirbt ein kurzer Verdacht.

And in the morning, you turn on the shower

And out comes . . . water, what did you think?

Red and blue stand for hot and cold.

The skin wasn't peeled off in strips like wallpaper.

That's just a nightmare, silly.

There's no thorn in the towel, no blood

On the tiles—the plug hole's gurgle

Signifies cleanliness, not death.

As to whether they still make soap

Out of bones, the foam drying

On the lines of your palms takes the fifth.

Dragged along by the hair, briefly, fear-

Fully animated, a short-lived suspicion dies.

›Jedes hängt seinen Gedanken nach‹
    War kein Motiv für soviel
Unterwegssein, blind für den Fakt, daß
    Auch dies sich vergißt. Bald
Wirst du völlig erledigt sein, rufen
    Die Jahre dem Staunenden zu.
Denn ganz ohne Prämien nimmt Leben
    Geschickt seinen Lauf. Aufzustehn
Morgens auf falschem Fuß, hochrot
    Mit den Hormonen im Fluß,
Ein anatomischer Torso vorm Spiegel,
    Die Arme im Anschlag, Augen
Weitaufgerissen . . . um *was* zu sehn?

"Everyone follows his or her own bent"
   Was really no excuse for so much time
On the road, oblivious to the fact
   That that, too, is fugitive. Before long,
You'll be completely done up and done in,
   The years call out to the peregrine.
Because life takes whatever course it will,
   Without inducements. You get out of bed
On the wrong side, lobster red
   With the hormones in your bloodstream,
An anatomical torso in the mirror,
   And you stand there, arms akimbo, eyes
Peeled . . . to see what?

Keiner, der nicht hofft . . . Und los geht's
    Hinein in den Abend, der bald
Vor dem Andrang zurückweicht, Straßen
    Auf Durchgang gestellt. Paradox
Das Gefühl, daß nichts fehlt, ohne dich.
    Wie jemand, weit abgeschlagen,
Zu spät bemerkt, daß alles ihm fremd ist,
    Schließt du dich schließlich
Dem murmelnden Draußen, dem Fließband,
    Der geräuschvollen Mehrheit an.
Während oben, im Regen, ein Rotlicht,
    Irgendein wippendes Frauenbein
Nach einer langen Nacht jäh verlischt.

No one without some expectation . . . and they're off
   Into the evening, which rapidly makes it-
Self scarce in the face of so much interest.
   Streets become thoroughfares. An irrational
Feeling that it's all complete without you.
   Like someone, miles adrift, noticing
Too late that everything round about him
   Is unfamiliar, you finally join in
The murmurous throng, the reciprocal
   Assembly line of the noisy majority.
Red lights sizzle in the rain, until
   The high-kicking legs in their canny cancan
Call it a night and go dark.

Unwirklich das Zimmer, allein bewohnt.
    Im Spiegel Insektendreck, Staub
In den Ecken, gesammelt um Frauenhaar,
    Das schon Wochen dort liegt.
Keine Früchteschale, keine Vase in Sicht,
    Die einzigen Füllhörner, dicht
Gerückt, Bücher. Was von Stilleben blieb,
    Von den kleinen Tropismen sind
Ganz banale Rätsel wie eine blaue . . . 13 . . . —
    Aufs Handgelenk tätowiert,
Wunden, aufgesprungen, ein Muttermal.
    Lächelnd und kaum entsetzt
Suchst du in alphabetischen Gebeten Halt.

Unreal the room you live in by yourself,
   The fly-spotted mirror, dust
In the corners clustering round a long hair
   That's been lying there for weeks.
No bowl of fruit, no vase,
   The only cornucopias, stacked tight,
Are the books. The only surviving elements
   Of the still life are little tropes,
Banal riddles like the blue 13
   Tattooed on your wrist,
Wounds, opened, a birthmark.
   Smiling and almost not at all appalled
You look to alphabetical charms for help.

Nachgiebig weich wie in den Kniekehlen
Fleisch — der begehrliche Traum
Wie er dem einzelnen zustößt, im Bett
Oder offenen Auges beim Gehn:
Etwas blitzt auf, macht sich rar, intrigiert,
Austernhaft kühl und feucht,
Um eine Falte, ein Büschel Flimmerhaar.
War es ein Gaumen, der Spalt
Eines Augenlids, wie in der Infrarotsicht
Wärme der Haut als Indiz für
Versteckte Leichen. Ein Hüftschwung reicht
Und von neuem beginnt was
So hinfällig endet, so wehrlos und weich.

As soft and yielding as the backs of your knees,
    The dream of desire that might come to you
Asleep in bed (*in your dreams!*),
    Or else wide-eyed, awake, walking:
A flash of something fleeting, captivating,
    Oysterishly cool and damp
Round a crease, a tuft of flamy hair.
    The pink of gums, maybe, or the crack
Of an eyelid, the infrared eye sniffs human warmth
    And infers interred bodies.
A shake of the hips will do it,
    And all over again something begins
That will end so staggeringly, so yieldingly and unresistingly.

Und dann die Umgebung, die Verstecke
　　Diskreter Leben, so einzeln,
Von Mängeln getrieben, gewinnverliebt
　　Daß man vergißt wie man herkam
In diese Häuser mit Tarnanstrich, Zeuge
　　Uralten und jüngsten Handels
Entlang der Ausfallstraßen aufs Land.
　　Besser den Körpern zu folgen
In ihrer Brownschen Bewegung, höflich
　　Phönizischen Regeln gehorchend
Statt den verbotnen Gerüchen, obszönen
　　Flüchen und diesem Singsang
Auf ein paar Wellenlängen seit Orpheus.

And then the surroundings, the hiding places
    Of separate lives, so single,
Driven by lack, by want, in love with winning
    That you forget how you got here,
Among these camouflaged houses that witnessed
    All the ancient and recent trades along
The arterial routes into the countryside.
    Better to follow the bodies
In their Brownian motion, politely
    Obeying Phoenician protocols,
Instead of the forbidden aromas, obscene
    Oaths, and this crooning available
On one or two frequencies since Orpheus.

Skeptisch, belesen, gereizt . . . ganz im Stil
    Der Annoncen, unendlich fern
Jeder Landschaft, mit wenigen Strichen
    Gezeichnet, der Zeitungsmensch
Mit dem Innern im Zwielicht, warst du.
    O diese Zartheit der Lungen . . .
Das Xylophon aus verborgenen Knochen
    Vom Schädel zum Kleinen Zeh.
Und daß die Körper schwer finden, was
    Ihr Begehren sucht, daß Gewalt
Sie in Schlingen zwingt, bis sie hastig,
    Aufgezehrt vom Geschwätz,
Zum Ausgang drängeln, — wohin damit?

Skeptical, well read, irritated . . . you were
    In the style of the small ads, infinitely remote
From any landscape limned
    In one or two strokes, the newspaper man
With his twilit soul, that was you.
    O the frailty of those lungs . . .
The xylophone of hidden bones
    From the cranium to the little toe.
The trouble bodies have finding
    What their desires seek, the violence
That forces them into its trammels, till,
    Hurriedly, eaten up with gossip,
They press toward the exit—what to do there?

Unsichtbar sein, sich geräuschlos im Raum
    Bewegend, ein Körper aus Luft,
Klinken drückend, wie animiert, Treppen
    Herauf- und heruntergleitend,
Wie an Spinnweb-Flaschenzügen sich leicht
    Durch Fenster hangelnd, ein Ariel
Ohne Auftrag und unter niemands Vaterblick,
    Im Dunkel der Kinos zu Hause,
In Bankkeller, Schiffskabine und Luxussuite,
    Ein blinder Passagier, wunschlos
Hinter gebauschtem Vorhang, vom Licht
    Unbehelligt, vom Wer-ist-Wer:
In einer Welt voller Totschlag — schnell weg.

To be invisible, moving silently
    In space, an ethereal body,
Turning doorknobs as though remote-controlled,
    Gliding upstairs and down,
Hanging out the window as though dangling
    On the spider's web of a block and tackle, an Ariel
Without orders and under no one's paternal eye,
    At home in tenebrous cinemas,
In bank vaults, ship's cabins, and luxury suites,
    A stowaway, lacking for nothing
Behind the billowing curtains, unaffected
    By the light, by the ship's manifest:
In a world of murder and mayhem—run for it.

Achtlos, wie alles anfängt, noch schläfrig
  Im Gähnen blutend, siehst du
Dein Kinn im Spiegel zerschnitten, die Haut
  Unterm Schwedenstahl frösteln,
Die Augen im Morgenlicht glasig, ein Tier
  Das den aufrechten Gang übt,
Den Gebrauch von Werkzeug. Wie Läuse,
  Im Waschbecken wimmelnd,
Die Stoppeln Barthaar, — mit jeder Rasur
  Kehrt das Feilschen wieder, sucht
Deine Angst den Balanceakt: ein erstes
  Plädoyer für das Unschuldsherz,
Lang vor dem Adernöffnen die Amnestie.

Negligently, the way everything begins,
    You yawn and bleed, you stare at
Your cut chin in the glass, the skin puckered
    Under the Swedish steel,
The eye glazed in the morning light, an animal
    In double jeopardy, practicing
The use of edged tools while standing on its hindlegs.
    The beard hairs swarm like lice
In the basin, and each time you shave
    The haggling begins again, your fear
Seeks an equilibrium: a first plea
    For the innocent heart,
The amnesty long before the opened veins.

Kurz vor Karfreitag packt dich der Schlaf
　Wie bei jedem Fest. Nichts
Stört den Ablauf der Tage. Blasphemisch
　Hörst du die Preßluft entweichen —
Irgendein Graben entsteht, ein Kaufhaus
　Lädt pünktlich zur Auferstehung
Mit neuen Preisen ein. Fast erleichtert
　Beschreibt ein Gerichtsbericht
Den Weinkrampf des Mörders, seinen Fleiß
　All die Jahre davor. Ostern
Bringt den Familien Arrest ein. Die Kinder
　Denken an Weihnachten. Bald
Gibt es Neujahrswünsche und Sekt um Zwölf.

Just before Good Friday, as before

    Every holiday, narcolepsy hits. Nothing

Disturbs the passing of the days. Blasphemously

    You hear the hydraulic hiss and thrum—

Some new premises coming into being, a department store

    Celebrates its resurrection with new prices.

Almost with relief, the law report

    Describes the killer breaking down in tears—

So much industry all those years ago.

    Easter quarantines family by family.

(The children are dreaming of Christmas.)

    Soon it will be time for first-footing,

Coals, and champagne at midnight.

Was für ein blutiger Knirps du mal warst,
    Ein runzliger Kobold, verknotet
Die Arme, die Beine. Mit bläulicher Haut
    Wie um dein Leben strampelnd,
Früh um dein künftiges Sterben bemüht.
    Und alles fing so untröstlich an
Mit einem gellenden Schrei, als die Welt
    In die Lungen zog, rasselnd.
Mit einem Schock (›Soviel Licht!‹), einem Schnitt
    Flinker Scheren und Messer
In das einzige Fleisch, das nicht du warst.
    Der Nabel erinnert den Faden,
Die Zerreißlust der Parzen von Anfang an.

What a bloody little leprechaun you once were,
    A wrinkled imp with knotted
Arms and legs. Bluish skin,
    As though kicking for your life,
Early concerned with your impending death.
    And it all began so unconsolably,
With a piercing yell, when the world
    Moved into your lungs with a rattle.
With a shock ("so much light!"), a slicing
    Of deft scissors and knives
Into the only flesh that wasn't you.
    The umbilicus was like the thread,
The Fates' love of sundering from the get-go.

Peinlich, — schon auf den frühesten Photos
   Dasselbe Lächeln voll Zutraun
Zum Objektiv, das die Strahlen bündelt
   In ein Nostalgia, geöffnet
Für Millisekunden, der Körper verführt
   Vom Versprechen der Wiederkehr
Der vertrauten Dinge. Und später ist Zeit
   Mit den Händen zu greifen,
Ein Schwinden, bestürzend, auf Zelluloid.
   Wie dein Lächeln sich auflöst
Beim Betrachten nach Jahren. Befangen
   Vom Unbekannten, fixiert auf
Längst Fernes, weist dein Blick dich zurück.

Embarrassing—the way even the earliest photographs
    Of you show the same trusting smile
At the lens, which bunches your beams
    Into a nostalgia, opened
For milliseconds, the body seduced
    By the promise of the return
Of everything familiar. And later
    Time is palpably passing,
A vanishing, shocking, on celluloid.
    Just as your smile seems to dissolve
As you look at it years later. Chary
    Of the unknown, fixed on something
Long ago and far away, your gaze rejects you.

Mannsdicke Rohre, in die du als Kind dich

    Im Versteckspiel verkrochst

Waren im nächsten Traum riesige Tunnel,

    Bunker und Tropfsteinhöhlen,

In denen du Urmensch warst oder Soldat . . .

    Doch vor allem erwachsen, voraus

Diesen schmächtigen Fesseln, der Ohnmacht

    Von Geschlecht und Statur. Flach

Auf den Wiesen warst du, von frischer Erde

    Betäubt, in den Mulden aus Gras

Dir selbst so nah wie die Birnen dem Stamm.

    Bis es galt, im Trikot zu gehn,

Freihändig pissend, die Schultern wattiert.

The thick lengths of piping you crawled into
    As a child in your games of hide-and-seek
Were enormous tunnels in the dreams that ensued,
    Bunkers, and limestone caverns,
Where you were a primitive man, or a soldier . . .
    But above all, you were grown up,
Slipped from your frail bonds of the feebleness
    Of your family and size. You lay flat on the meadows,
Stunned by the overwhelming smell of earth,
    As close to yourself in the grassy hollow,
As a pear to the pear tree.
    Till it was time to wear the team shirt,
And piss—look, no hands—in padded shoulders.

Denn was heißt schon Kindheit, nach Jahren
Der Flucht, ein erpreßter Wunsch,
Sprungbereit auf den Lippen, ein Kehrreim
Wie Heimat und Komm-nach-Haus.
Über die Schultern gespuckt, war das fatale
Zurücksehn ein schlechter Tausch
Für das Kürzerwerden von Tag und Nacht.
Verwaschen die Farben, die rosa
Idyllen aus Lammfell. Das war's: der Geruch
Erbrochener Milch, das Komplott
Großer Körper, die dich fütternd erdrückten,
Ganze Wolken von Hysterie,
In denen man laufen lernte und sich zu wehrn.

What is childhood anyway, after years
    Of running away, an extorted wish
Quivering on your lips, a nursery chant
    Like home and belonging.
Spat over your shoulder the deadly look
    Back was a poor exchange
For the shrinking of both day and night.
    The colors washed out, the pink idyll
Of lambskin. That was it: the whiff
    Of regurgitated milk, the conspiracy
Among the growns to feed and stifle you,
    Great clouds of hysteria
Where you learned to walk, and to fight back.

Seltsam, woran sich das Auge gewöhnt.
   Der geschlossene Horizont
Rings, und wo Fleisch war, das Dunkel
   Im Röntgenbild, helle Flocken
Für Mark und Bein. Noch beim Liebesakt
   Tropft das Rosa aus, rangeln
Die Körper in Einzelgliedern, tranchiert.
   Und der Blick ist schon kalt
Bevor das Leben erkaltet. Die seltne Lust
   Sich betastet zu fühlen, wach
Unterm Messer zu liegen, wird glitzernd
   Von Tropfen quittiert, Tränen
In denen die Freude sich sammelt als Rest.

Strange, the things an eye can get used to:
    The sealed rim of the horizon
On every side, and the substitution
    On X-ray photographs, of black for flesh,
Light flecks for bone and marrow.
    Even in the act of love, the pink leaks out,
The bodies are a tangle of individual limbs.
    And the eye goes cold even before life chills.
An unaccountable yen to be palped,
    To lie under the knife, and awake,
Is repaid by glittering droplets,
    Tears in which joy collects:
A residue, an overplus, a meniscus.

Wie viele Gesten sind sinnlos, und dennoch
  Hält ein Staunen sie wach. Wütend
Einer Fliege zu drohen, in steifer Andacht
  Vor den Toten den Kopf zu senken,
Mit Grüßen und Winks sich die Einzelhaft
  Zu versüßen, kann amüsant
Oder anständig sein. Vor der Trägheit
  Der Wolken wird alles absurd.
Niemand sieht diesen Clown sich betrügen.
  Den Zeugen, kurz eingenickt,
Ist der Lidschlag entgangen, der Hinweis
  Gespreizter Finger, wenn List
Im Verkehr der Indizien die Zunge löst.

How many gestures are futile, and yet
    Their inadequacy keeps them going.
To make menaces at a fly, to lower the head
    In mute respect before the departed,
To sweeten your time in solitary by waving
    Or greeting, can be diverting
Or decent. It's all absurd anyway,
    Against the slothful clouds.
No one sees the clown making an ass of himself.
    The witnesses nodded off, and missed
The blink of an eye, the expression
    Of a spread hand, when cunning
In the presence of proof loosens the tongue.

Was für ein Händepaar, was für ein Blatt
    Noten, ein verstimmtes Klavier,
Spielt da zusammen und du hörst nur dies:
    Üble Etüden im Vorraum
Zu einer der Ängste, einer der Kammern,
    Verboten, wie Uhrkästen eng.
Auf geschlossenen Deckeln die Schlüssel
    Für Überdruß, für den Rumor
In Bauchhöhlen . . . Was für ein Taktzähler,
    Was für Gesang? Feiner Sand
Rinnt aus den Rasseln, den Fetischmasken
    Auf staubige Tasten. Hörst du
In welcher Enge du atmest, dich regst?

The identity of the hands, the piece of sheet music,
    The out-of-tune piano,
Are unknown to you, you know only:
    Bad études in the anteroom
To one of your fears, one of your chambers,
    Verboten, tight as a grandfather clock.
On closed lids, the keys for
    Excess, for the rumbling of tummies . . .
What metronome, what vocal?
    Fine sand spills out of the rattle,
The fetish masks on the dusty keys.
    Do you hear the constriction
In which you live and breathe?

Daß es die Dinge sind, die dich verhöhnt,
  Schwindend im Tageslicht,
Dir selbst überlassen, daß Zeit sich zuerst
  An Lebendiges hält, Lächeln
Noch unwägbar, Nacken und feines Haar:
  Seit wann siehst du, wie weit
Dieses Einstweilen reicht, was den Möbeln
  Die Wette gilt? Aus der Sicht
Eines Stuhlbeins ist jeder Tisch ein Sarg,
  Unverrückbar im Schattenreich
Hinterbliebener Mieter, in dem Bewohner
  Längst Tote sind, auf Besuch.
Wie die Vase sich ausschweigt, die Klinke.

That it's things that have made a mockery
    Of you, fading away into the daylight
Left to your own devices; that time goes after living
    Things first, imponderable smiles,
The backs of necks and hair-fine hair;
    How long since you first saw
How far the past extends that the furniture
    Stakes its life on? From the vantage point
Of a chair leg, every table is a coffin,
    Immovable in the shadow realm
Of former tenants, residents long since dead,
    Paying nostalgic visits. Listen
To the tight-lipped vase, the laconic doorknob.

Unmöglich zu fliegen — mit dieser Brust,
   Flach wie bei Emu und Strauß.
Zu sperrig die Rippen und ohne Schwung
   Die Gelenke, nicht leicht genug.
Stehst du am Fenster, Arme verschränkt,
   Den Möwen im Sturzflug folgend,
Ist es wie Zahnschmerz, und jeder Bogen,
   Jedes Und, jede Rundung läßt dich
Am Boden zurück, Exemplar einer Tierart
   Vom Rückfall bedroht, Invalid
Mit gestrecktem Hals. Nur ein Pinguin
   Hält es aus im Stehn, am Rand,
Unter Flügelzucken und schwerem Traum.

Fat chance of taking to the air with a chest
    As flat as an ostrich's or emu's.
Too much bulk on the ribs, insufficient momentum
    In the limbs, not enough lightness.
As you stand by the window with folded arms,
    Watching the gulls plummet and curvet,
It feels like toothache, and every swoop
    And curve and conjunction leaves you
Earthbound, an instance of a species
    Threatened with relapse, an invalid
With a cricked neck. Only a penguin
    Can stand to stand on the brink, stand to
With wing shrugs and heavy dreams.

Und was ist es sonst, als Magie, dieser Riß
   Zwischen Namen und Dingen,
Als einziges Echolot ins Verbotne: Tabus?
   Wie eine Hand, abgetrennt,
Unterm Tisch liegt ein ledriges Kaktusblatt,
   Kahl auf dem Teller die Gräte,
Einer Haarspange ähnlich in kaltem Fett.
   Daß man die Toten herausputzt,
Erzählt auf dem Bügel die Hose, das Hemd
   Über den Stuhl gelegt, nachts.
Ein Eimer vergrößert den Raum, eine Lupe
   Die feinen Risse im Schädeldach.
. . . Bilder wie Grabbeigaben an jeder Wand.

What else is it but magic, that chasm
　　Between things and their names,
The only echo sounding into the forbidden realm
　　Of the taboo? A leathery cactus leaf
Lies under the table like a severed hand,
　　A bare fishbone on the plate
Resembles a hairclip in a pool of grease.
　　The idea that you doll up the dead
Is something the trousers say in their press,
　　The shirt draped over the chair back at night.
A bucket makes its contribution to available space,
　　A magnifying glass scrutinizes the crazed cranium.
Paintings like grave ornaments on every wall.

Grundlos, wie Leben entsteht, ist es bereit
    Zu vergehn in den Kehlen,
Durch die Finger zu rinnen, die Wand hinab.
    Was sich nie ausging, war Angst.
In jeder Kneipe zu haben, am rechten Fleck
    War es der Dampf an der Theke,
Der Geruch von geschlachteten Hühnern
    Aus Küchen, das ranzige Öl,
Das Zerkochen von Meeresfrüchten zu Müll.
    Schaudernd siehst du den Krebs
Mit verbundenen Scheren, Forelle und Aal
    Unterm Schlammbauch des Karpfen.
Im Kofferraum schreit eine Katze nach Luft.

As providentially as life comes into being
    It's ready to go again, in your throat,
Between your fingers, dribbling down the walls.
    What remained constant was fear.
On offer in every diner, in the right spot
    It was the steam issuing over the bar,
The smell of dead chicken from the kitchen,
    The rancid oil, the boiling
Of shellfish to fertilizer. With a shudder
    You see the crab with rubber bands
Round its claws, the trout and eel nuzzling
    The slimy belly of the vast carp.
A cat cries in the car trunk for air.

Und oft wird auf halbem Wege der Tod
    Unterbrochen, bevor er selbst
Unterbricht, — eine Stockung im Kreislauf,
    Aufschwünge, Stürze, Bedauern
Wegen so vieler Enden, so vieler Beginne
    Wie es Reflexe gibt, Wechsel
Der Ansichten zwischen Amöbe und Stern.
    Das Einzeln-, das Irre-
Das Spaltungsirresein täuscht sich gewitzt
    Vor zerbrochenen Spiegeln
In der Pose Vergeßlichkeit: jede Lücke
    Ein verlorenes Fundstück,
Die Mühe, es wiederzufinden, ein Psalm.

And often death itself is interrupted half-
    Way, before it can effect its own
Interruption—a blockage in an artery,
    Leaps up, downfalls, commiserations
Over as many endings, as many beginnings
    As there are reflexes, changes
Of opinion between amoeba and astra.
    The weariness of vagaries,
Of singularities, of the versions of fission,
    Cleverly tricks itself out
In broken mirrors in the pose of forgetfulness:
    Every crack is a missing piece,
And the effort of finding it is a psalm.

Um von vorn zu beginnen, — der Anfang
    Liegt in den Tagen danach,
In den Zweifeln der Frau, wem die Wucht
    Dieses Andrangs galt. Möglich,
Daß ihre Echos ihr fremd sind am Morgen,
    Das Neue, zu früh in Sicht,
Sie erpreßt und zur Umkehr zwingt, Panik,
    Daß ihre Zeit nun vorbei ist.
Was ist sein Stöhnen gegen die Sprengung
    In ihrem Innern, den Schwindel,
Daß der Rhythmus gestört ist, ihr Zögern
    Eh das Ei seinen Ort erreicht,
Die Furcht vor dem Ende, das nun beginnt.

To start over—isn't the true beginning
   In the days immediately ensuing,
In the woman's wondering who was the object
   Of such forceful suit. Possibly
Her echoes sound alien to her by the morning,
   The new life, glimpsed prematurely,
Blackmails her and forces her to turn back,
   In panic that her own life is over.
What are his groans, compared to
   The devastation wrought within her,
The disruption of her rhythm, her hesitation
   Before the egg reaches its hill station,
Her fear of the ending, shortly beginning.

Sieh, wie oft du zurückzuckst, gespiegelt
 Im Lackglanz von Kühlerhauben,
In metallischen Sonnenbrillen, dir selbst
 Widerfahrend in einer Drehtür,
Die dich hineinzieht. So schnell vervielfacht,
 Warst du immer schon vor dir da
Wie der Igel im Märchen, lästiges Visavis.
 Hämisch auf Fettaugen treibend,
In jeder Suppe zur Stelle, in jedem Bier,
 Gab es nicht viel zu viele von dir?
Stand nicht noch immer in jedem Tröpfchen
 Eins deiner Doubles, im Zweifel
Ob Zeit wirklich sämtliche Züge verwischt.

Observe how often you flinch from your re-
    Flection on the lacquered metal of car hoods,
In reflector sunglasses, on encountering
    Yourself in a revolving door
That spins you in. So rapidly replicated,
    You were always there ahead of yourself
Like the hedgehog in the fairy tale, an irritating
    Opposite number. Drifting malignantly
On eyes of fat in soup, in every glass of beer,
    Were there not always too many of you?
Was there not always one of your doubles
    In every droplet, making you wonder
Whether time really did cover its traces.

Denk von den Wundrändern her, vom Veto
   Der Eingeweide, vom Schweigen
Der Schädelnähte. Das Aufgehn der Monde
   Über den Nagelbetten führt
Andere Himmel herauf, strenger gestirnt.
   Lachhaft die Höhenflüge, getrübt
Aus den engen Knochenhöhlen der Ausblick
   Auf Kloaken und Gräberreihen,
Hautflecken, zyklisch, und Sternbilder, nah.
   Weiter ist hier die Umlaufbahn,
Länger dauert es in den kälteren Nächten
   Bis die Blutung gestillt ist, Hunger
Den Körper versiegelt, das Schwarze Loch.

Think from the rim of wounds, from the veto
    Of the intestines, the silence
Of the cranial seams. The moonrise
    Of your fingernails adduces
Other heavens more sternly starred.
    Strange the flights, the dim view
From narrow bone arches
    Of cloacas and tombstones,
Scraps of skin, cyclical and constellations at hand.
    The orbit is more generous here,
It takes longer on chillier nights
    For the bleeding to be stanched,
And hunger to tamp the body, the black hole.

Lange her, daß dein Finger ein Halt war,
    Ein Laufsteg hinaus in die Luft,
Für den Sänger von Theben, das Heupferd,
    Die rasenden Maikäferhorden,
Den Hopliten am Feldrand, die Schildlaus.
    Immer färbten die Flügel ab
Der ermüdeten Schmetterlinge, Papyri
    Mit Hieroglyphen beschmiert. Kot
War die Schleifspur der Raupenkolonnen.
    Blattgrüner Hügel, der Daumen
Blutig vom Rumpf der zerdrückten Mücke.
    In den Handrücken brannte
Eine vom Fußvolk, die Ameise, sich ein.

It's a long time since your finger was a crutch,

    A walkway into the air

For the singer of Thebes, the green grasshopper,

    The wild hordes of june bugs,

The hoplites on the edge of the field, the shield louse.

    The wings always bleached

On tired butterflies, papyrus streaked

    With hieroglyphs.

Dirt marked the route of the caterpillar colonies.

    Greeny hills, the thumb bloodied

From the body of the squashed mosquito.

    On the back of your hand, meanwhile,

One of the ant-sappers was digging in.

Solange noch Gras sprießt aus allen Fugen
    Ist nichts verloren. Der Baum
Mißt die Menschenalter in kleinen Ringen.
    Von einer Wohnung für viele
Bleibt im Brandfall nur ein verkohltes Loch
    Oder ein schöner Spielplatz. Leicht
Steigt im Stadtwind aus Abgas ein Drachen,
    Fährt auf den aschenen Pfützen
Ein Schiff aus Papier. Wie dein Herz springt,
    Wenn die schimpfende Amsel
Ihr Stück Rasen verteidigt am Straßenrand,
    Und überall grünt es. Der Schritt
Federt oft über Gräbern, planiert zum Weg.

Nothing is lost, not while grass sprouts
    From every crack. The tree
Measures human life in little rings.
    Of an apartment block, in the event of fire,
Only a charred hole will remain,
    Or a kids' playground. A kite soars aloft
In the city's updraft of pollution,
    A paper boat in a puddle
Sets keel to breakers. How your heart leaps
    To hear the scolding blackbird
Defend her patch of lawn by the side of the road,
    And green everywhere. Your walk takes you
Over graves, knocked down to pathway.

Doch der wahre Spuk war das Einmaleins
  Das die Träume in Netze legte,
Tagtäglich, das Schwirren von Bumerangs
  Um die zahllosen Dinge, der Zwang
Zu Gemenge und Handlung, das Rechnen
  Im Schlaf, algebraisch gelähmt.
Seit du, ein Häkchen, stumm überm Heft,
  Ziffern in Kästchen sperrtest
Bist du selbst dieses vielfache Ganze, geteilt
  In sezierbare Glieder, der Kopf
Zwischen Minus und Plus, Haut und Hirn
  So unendlich gefaltet. Die Tage
Gezählt, wird das Leben zum Intervall.

But the real terror was the times table
  That enmeshed your dreams,
Day after day the whirring of boomerangs
  Around the innumerable things, the compulsion
To engagement and action, counting
  In your sleep, the algebraic crippling.
Ever since you, a little squiggle, mute over your exercise book,
  Locked figures up in little boxes,
You yourself have become this multiple whole,
  Divided into integral parts, the head
Havering between positive and negative,
  Skin and brow so infinitely pleated. Your days
Numbered, your life became an interval.

Fröstelnd unter den Masken des Wissens,
  Von Unerhörtem verstört,
Traumlos am Tag unter zynischen Uhren,
  Fahrplänen, Skalen, beraten
Von fröhlichen Mördern, vorm Monitor, —
  So wird man Sarkast. Fest
Steckt im Zähneknirschen die Reduktion,
  Im Mangel die Schadenfreude,
In Monologen aus Irrsinn das süße Singen
  Des Kinds, von zu Hause entflohn
Aus der Stadt, querfeldein, auf die Dörfer,
  Wo die Füße nachts schmerzten,
Der Augengrund, von Insekten bewohnt.

Shivering under masks of knowledge,
    Freaked out by the extraordinary,
Dreamless by day under cynical clocks,
    Timetables, scales, counseled by
Cheerful killers, in front of the monitor—
    It made you sarcastic. Gripped
In the gritted teeth is diminution,
    Malevolence in shortage,
In a scatty monologue the sweet songs
    Of the child, run away from home
And city, over the fields to villages
    Where your feet throb at night,
The backs of your eyes peopled by monsters.

Die Nerven blank wie unter Flügeldecken,
  Genügt ein kreischender Baukran
Am Mittag, dich zu erschrecken, ein Pfiff
  Ums Eck, eine zischende Dose.
In diesem jüngsten Himmel-Hölle-Spiel
  Bricht etwas auf, sprengt Risse
Ins alte Hirngewölbe des Jahrhunderts.
  Der Boden dröhnt. Sixtinisch
Hallt es von musealen Stunden, tickend
  Im Zentrum, über leere Plätze.
Derselbe Kalk, der die Schlagadern engt,
  Drängt die Straßen ins Weite,
Scheidet die Geister vor einer Hochhauswand.

Your nerves worn smooth as under wing cases,
    It takes just a screaking crane at noon
To make you jump, a whistle
    Round the corner, the hiss of a ring-pull.
In this latest confrontation of heaven and hell,
    Something bursts asunder, causes cracks to run
Through the old brain arch of the century.
    The ground rumbles. Sistine echoes
Resound from museum hours,
    Ticking across empty squares.
The same lime that narrows the arteries
    Drives the roads out into the countryside,
Parts the spirits in front of a skyscraper wall.

Und immer das Warten auf den Transport
    Zwischen den Orten, wo Ankunft
Ein Portal ist im Regen, ein weißer Flugplatz
    Der sofort Abschied meint: Exit
Durch ein Tageskino, ein helles Nachtcafé,
    Vorbei an den Förderbändern
Mit raunenden Koffern, Taschen, vertauscht.
    Niemand da, der dich auffängt,
Trittst du zeitkrank ins Freie, schwankend
    Vor Raumnot, ein Evakuierter,
Den ein Taxi holt aus der Zone des Bebens
    Ins Hotel, vor die Schalterhallen,
Wo Zugluft ihn abschiebt aufs nächste Gleis.

And always the waiting for transport
    From here to there, where arrival
Is a doorway in the rain, and a white airport
    Spells immediate departure: you exit
Through a 24-hour cinema, a perma-neon café,
    Past conveyor belts murmuring
With the plausible luggage of others.
    No one there to meet you,
You step, jet-lagged, into the open, reeling
    With the memory of claustrophobia,
An evacuee by taxi from the earthquake zone
    To your hotel, to the *salle des pas perdus*,
Where a sudden updraft dispatches you to the nearest track.

Auch der kälteste Raum wird zur Sauna,
  Solange du irrläufst. Wie steil
Führt ins Erdreich die Treppe, wie streng
  Der Geruch ist, die Trennung
In *Damen* und *Herren* . . . Die falsche Tür,
  Kaum berührt, lockt ins Abseits,
In verbotne Zonen, vor Wände, markiert
  Mit den Zoten der Gegenseite.
Nichts macht so einsam wie das Geschlecht.
  In Kabinen gesperrt, lauschend
Der stygischen Spülung, den Eingeweiden,
  Allein mit dem Ekel, der Lust,
Klebt an den Fliesen der Körper und träumt.

The coldest room becomes a sauna
   To your straying. How steeply the steps
Lead down into the earth's interior, how choking
   The smell, how strict the separation
Of Ladies and Gentlemen . . . The wrong door,
   No sooner touched, leads you astray,
To forbidden zones, to walls scribbled
   With the witty obscenities of the other side.
Nothing so confining as gender.
   Locked into cubicles, all ears to the pump,
The Stygian flush, the bowels and bowls,
   Alone with disgust and desire,
The body pressed dreaming to the tiles.

Gut zu wissen, daß Schwarz die Dinge hält,
  Daß es die Blicke beschlagnahmt,
Ein letzter Zoll, verläßlich wie nie ein Blau.
  Kein Verröcheln der Farben, kein
Quälender Schmerz, nur ein einfaches Aus,
  Ohne Widerhall. Armes Klavier,
Das die Töne verspiegelt in seiner Politur.
  Jedes Tuch behält mehr für sich.
Der heiße Asphalt zieht die Fußspuren ein
  Der Passanten des Sommers. Nein,
Selten ein Schwarz, das den Tod absorbiert,
  Die Blutlachen aufleckt, das Licht,
Diese letzte Zuflucht der Nerven, begräbt.

Good to know that black preserves things,
   That it compels the eye, a last customs post,
More dependable than any blue.
   No splutter of color, no
Torment, just a simple exit
   Without sostenuto. Poor piano,
Distorting the notes in its varnish.
   Every cloth keeps more for itself.
The hot asphalt holds the footprints
   Of the summer's pedestrian. No,
It's a rare black that absorbs death,
   Licks up the puddles of blood, entombs
.The light, last refuge of the nerves.

Wußten wir, was den Reigen in Gang hält?
    Daß Lieben einsamer macht,
Schien erwiesen. Jeder behielt ihn für sich,
    Seinen Dorn, bis zur Unzeit
Das Blut die Verbände durchschlug. Selten
    Blieb jemand unverletzt. Eher kroch
Ein Schmerz beim andern unter. Verlassen
    Zu sein war das größte Übel,
Nichts zu fühlen im Frühling, wie amputiert
    Vor defekten Riesenrädern . . .
Wie uns der Wind in die Baumkronen hob,
    Aus denen wir fallen sollten,
Glücklich, mit einem langen Himmelsschrei.

Did we know what makes the world go round?
    That love tends to isolate
Seemed clear enough. Everyone kept it for himself,
    His personal thorn, till the blood
Soaked through at the worst possible moment.
    It was rare for anyone to remain uninjured.
More commonly, the pain transferred itself
    To the other party. To be left
Was the worst evil, to be insentient in spring,
    Stand like an amputee under the busted
Ferris wheel . . . The way the wind carried us
    Into the treetops from which
We were later to fall with blissful cries.

Ging das meiste nicht spurlos an dir vorbei
    Ins Schweigen? Kaum aufzuhalten,
Der ferne Wolkenzug, der verregnete Tag,
    Ein Unfall, der tödlich endet.
Und jede Krise fing an mit dir. Du selbst
    Warst der eine zuviel im Stau.
Um dich her den erstaunlichen Schauplatz
    Verdunkeln Affekte. Ein Schock
Hellt ihn auf. In Gesprächen fließt Zeit ab,
    Beim Händewaschen, beim Essen.
Vor den Grausamkeiten schützt das Gebet,
    Das Idol vor der Zugluft —
Ein Gesicht, gealtert, kaum taucht es auf.

Did most of it not pass you by without trace,
  Into silence? Hardly to be stopped,
The faraway cloud formation, the rainy day,
  The accident with the fatal consequence.
And every crisis began with you.
  It was you that caused the gridlock.
In the remarkable scene around you
  Feelings darken. A shock lights it again.
Time flows by, in conversations,
  Washing your hands, over supper.
Prayer wards off the worst atrocities,
  The idol shielded from the dangerous draft—
A face pops up, already aged.

Ahnst du, wie überfüllt dieser Luftraum ist
　Mit Stimmen und Staub, schwirrend
Durch die Tiefen der Zeit. War die Libelle
　Von den Propellern des Weltkriegs
Ein Splitter? Tanzte der Mückenschwarm
　Sein Ballett nicht im Magnetfeld?
In den windkalten Korridoren der Straßen
　Erfaßt dich, noch aus der Ferne,
Der wache Dohlenblick. Aus dem Geraschel
　Des Laubs steigt der alte Disput
Theologischer Thesen. Zitternd verfehlst du
　Den einzelnen Kiesel, den Grashalm,
Die Umarmung der Erde, gefährlich wie nie.

Can you guess how overcrowded this space is
    With dust and voices, swirling
Through the depths of time. Was the dragonfly
    A splinter from the propellers
Of the Great War? Did the swarm of midges
    Not perform their ballet in a magnetic field?
In the windy corridors of the street,
    Still far off, a beady jackdaw
Marks you down. Out of the rustling of leaves
    Rises the ancient dispute
Of theological theses. Trembling,
    You miss the one pebble, the single
Blade of grass, earth's embrace, deadly as ever.

Waren es Augen wie diese, in denen das Fieber zuerst
Ausbrach, das große ›Oho‹, wortreich von Reue gefolgt?
Was für ein Sprung, was für ein Riesensatz aus dem Dickicht,
Von diesem Schimpansen zu Buster Keatons traurígem Blick
Über die Reling, dem Hut nach, unerreichbar im Wasser.
Und die Entfernung nimmt zu! Mit jedem neuen Unfall
Wird die Wirbelsäule ein wenig steifer, halten die Hände
Das Steuer fester inmitten der Trümmerhaufen aus Rädern
Und Blech, zerquetscht. Schon damals dasselbe Mißgeschick,
Derselbe hektische *slapstick*. Mit nacktem Arsch voran
Zurück in die kleinen Paradiese zu friedensstiftendem Sex.
O weh, diese Trauer, geboren zu sein und nicht als Tier,
Die böse Vergeblichkeit, hingenommen mit unbewegtem Gesicht.

Was it in eyes like these that the fever first flickered,
The great Aha, followed by voluminous remorse?
What a giant step from the jungle, what a leap
From this chimpanzee to Buster Keaton's sad eyes
Over the railing, gazing after his hat in the water.
And the distance growing! With every fresh mishap
The spine stiffens a little more, the hands grip the wheel harder
In the smoking wreckage of rubber and steel.
Even then the same error-proneness,
The same hectic slapstick. And so, sidle back
To the little paradise for pacifying sex with the missus.
Oh, the sorrow to be born as not an animal,
The forlornness, accepted with expressionless features.

Daß eine Stahltür sich öffnet, und seinen letzten Käfig
Betritt ein Fabeltier, zitternd, weil es Zeit ist zum Füttern,
Weil der Pfleger nach Hause will und das Publikum lacht,
Steht in keiner der Einhorn-Legenden verzeichnet. Okapi, —
Ein Wort aus den Urwaldsprachen, die niemand mehr spricht.
Zu kurz für Savannen, hat dieser geduldige, rostbraune Hals
Die Strohballen verdient, den vergitterten Schlafstall.
Denn die gerodete Welt wird ihm fremd sein, so fremd
Wie dem zerstreuten Besucher ein kombiniertes Tier,
Halb Giraffe, halb Zebra, und von den kindlichen Schatten,
Den Bilderbuch-Silhouetten beider, gleich weit entfernt.
Noch so ein Wiederkäuer verlorener Zeiten, ein Posten
Am zoologischen Wegrand aufgestellt, wie zur Warnung
Vor der Exotik von Hinterbliebenen, einsam in ihrer Art.

The clank of a steel door, and the ignominious entrance
Of the heraldic beast, trembling, because it's feeding time,
And the keeper wants to knock off, and the beastly onlookers are
    laughing…
These are things not writ in any unicorn legend. Okapi—
The word is from jungle languages, now themselves extinct.
Insufficiently tall for the savannah, this patient, rust-colored
Throat merits its pellets of straw, and its locked stall at night.
Because the free range world will be strange to him,
As strange as to the bemused visitor
This combination of giraffe and zebra,
Equally remote from the familiar child cutout of either.
One more ruminant from the olden days, a sentry
Planted on the zoological roadside, as though to warn
Against the pathos of the exotic throwback.

Für gewöhnlich fängt es mit Kunststücken an. Eine Tierschau
Präsentiert die geordneten Reihen, Kokarden nach vorn:
Seehunde im Trio, Bälle jonglierend auf ihren Nasen, schlanke
Wendige Statuen, von Dompteuren synchron geschaltet
Wie am Broadway die Tänzer, in den Ghettos die Eckensteher,
Schlaksig verrenkt vor den Feuerleitern. Dann erst kam er,
Dieser junge Pinguin mit dem Namen des deutschen Gelehrten,
Der einfach nur dastand, nichts konnte, nichts wollte, der Held
Früher Vaudevilles, flackernder Filmkomödien, schwarzweiß
Gezeichnet, den Stufen preisgegeben, der windschiefen Welt.
Heimlicher Favorit einer Minderheit kindlicher Wähler,
War er im Frack der Hotelportier, am Beckenrand schwankend,
Fröstelnd auf Schwimmflossen, die Flügel zuckend. Wie elend,
Vollendet sein Nichtstun, bis in den Abgang, ganz ohne Knicks.

It generally begins with tricks. An animal show
With the serried ranks, eyes and medals front:
A trio of seals, juggling balls on their noses, slim
Flexi-statues, synchronized by their trainers
Like Broadway chorines, or men mooching on street corners,
Lissomely draped around fire escapes. And then he came,
This young penguin with the name of a German philosopher,
Who just stood there, didn't do anything, couldn't do anything,
A hero of early vaudeville, of flickering black-and-white
Comedies, imperiled by flights of steps, by a windy world.
Secret favorite of a minority of the childish electorate,
He was the butler in tails, teetering on the brink of the pool,
Shivering on his flippers, swishing his wings. His performance
Faultlessly abject, down to the exit, sloping off, without a bow.

FROM

NACH DEN SATIREN

(1999)

(*NORMANDIE*)

Eingefallen am Bahndamm,
Liegt ein Hundekadaver quer im Gebiß
Kreideweiß numerierter Schwellen, erstarrt.

Je länger du hinsiehst, je mehr
Zieht sein Fell in den Staub ein, den Schotter
Zwischen den Inseln aus frischem Gras.

Dann ist auch dieses Leben, ein Fleck,
Gründlich getilgt.

(*NORMANDY*)

The body of a dead dog lies
Slumped on a railway embankment, chewed up
Among the chalk-numbered sleepers.

The longer you look, the more
His skin merges with the dirt, the pools
Of gravel in among the emerald grass.

And then the stain also of this life
Is finally laundered away.

(AUF GOTLAND)

Nur dies gab es auf lange Sicht hier, diesen Wellenfluß
Von Landschaft, fokussiert in einem Bussardauge, —
Die kahlen Hügel, einen Feldweg und am Rand
Die Hasenpfote im Gebüsch, vom Wind zerzaust
Ein abgenagtes Sprunggelenk, das in der Hand
So leicht wog wie ein Vogeljunges,
Das noch beweglich war, noch warm war und heraus
Sprang aus der Pfanne, blutig wie die Beute
Des Grauen Würgers auf dem Dorn der Eberesche, —
Ein kleiner Knöchel, winkend mit dem Fetzchen Fell.

Sah so der Rest von einem Hasen aus, nachdem
Der Schatten eines Flügels über ihn gekommen war,
Den Zickzacklauf ein Krallengriff, den flachen Atem
Gezielter Schnabelhieb beendet hatte? Unbequem
Muß dieser Tod gewesen sein, auf winterlicher Erde
Wehrlos verrenkt, die letzte Zuckung.
Was vom Gemetzel übrigblieb, hing in den Zweigen,
Die sich an nichts erinnern wie bestochne Zeugen.
Das Gras, längst wieder aufgerichtet, sorgt dafür,
Daß es auf lange Sicht nur dies gab hier, den Hasenfuß.

IN THE PROVINCES II

(*IN GOTLAND*)

From a distance, this was all there was to see,
An undulating landscape assembled in a buzzard's eye,
The bare hills, a track and at the edge of it
A rabbit's foot in the undergrowth, riffled by the wind,
A well-gnawed ankle joint that weighed no more
In the hand than a baby bird,
Still moving, still warm, that leaped
Out of the frying pan, bloodied as the prey
Of the gray butcher bird, on the rowan spike—
A little lump of bone beckoning with a flap of fur.

That was all that was left of a rabbit
Once the shadow of a wing crossed its path,
After its zigzag dash had been cut off by a claw, its panting
Breath by a well-aimed beak. How comfortless
This death must have been, helplessly splayed
On the wintry earth, the last convulsions.
The sole survivor of the slaughter perched in the boughs;
Like a bribed witness, it had no recollection of anything.
The grass, which had long since picked itself up, sees to it
That this was all there was to see, this rabbit's foot.

(*BÖHMEN*)

Die Stille um einen toten Maulwurf
Am Rand eines Weizenfeldes, sie trügt.
Unter ihm sammeln sich Käfer, bewaffnete Kräfte
In schwarzer Uniform. Über ihm kreist,
Bevor er abdreht, die Flügel zerzaust, ein Habicht.
Ameisen graben, Kommandos im Eilmarsch,
Am Rückgrat entlang eine Rinne. Im Innern
Laufen die Drähte heiß, wimmeln nervöse Maden
An der Börse der Eingeweide. Vom Bauchfell
Tragen fliegende Händler (oder sind es Reporter)
Die Botschaft in alle vier Winde: Ein Aas, ein Aas!
Nur eine Grille, einen Sprung weit entfernt,
Liest in den Wolkenzügen und sonnt sich
Schweigend, ein stoischer Philosoph.

(BOHEMIA)

The silence round a dead mole
On the edge of a wheat field is deceptive.
Under it is a rendezvous for beetles, armed
And in black. Above it wheels a hawk
With ruffled wings, till he veers away.
Like sappers at the double, ants dig
A trench along the spine. On its inside
The wires are glowing, nervous maggots
On the ticker tape. From the stomach lining
Traders in colored jackets (or are they reporters)
Carry the news to all parts: carrion, carrion!
Only a grasshopper, a hop and a skip away,
Scans the clouds and suns itself in the silence
Of a stoical philosopher.

(*CAMPANIA*)

Wie der Gekreuzigte lag dieser Frosch
Plattgewalzt auf dem heißen Asphalt
Der Landstraße. Offenen Mauls,

Bog sich zum Himmel, von Sonne gedörrt,
Was von fern einer Schuhsohle glich —
Ein Amphibium aus älterer Erdzeit,
Unter die Räder gekommen im Sprung.

Keine Auferstehung als in den Larven
Der Fliegen, die morgen schlüpfen werden.

Durch welche Öffnung entweicht der Traum?

IN THE PROVINCES IV

(*CAMPAGNA*)

A cruciform frog
Lay flattened against the hot macadam
Of the country lane. Mouth gaping

It curled heavenwards, dried out by the sun,
The sole of a shoe, as first appeared—
An amphibious holdout from an older era
Now caught under the wheels.

No resurrection, save in the form of the larvae
Of the flies that will hatch from it tomorrow.

The dream leaks out of which orifice?

(BEI AQUINCUM)

Wie vom Reisewagen gestreift eines fliehenden Siedlers
Lag auf der Römerstraße die tote Amsel, zerfetzt.

Einer, der immer dabei war, den nie was anging, der Wind
Hatte aus Flügelfedern ein schwarzes Segel gesetzt.

Daran erkanntest du sie, von fern, die beiseitegefegte,
Beim Einfall der Horde an die Erde geschmiegte Schwester.

Ob Daker und Hunnen, Mongolenpferde und Motorräder —
Schimpfend hatte sie abgelenkt von der Nähe der Nester.

Mehr war nicht drin. Sieht aus, als sei sie gleich hin gewesen.
Der miserablen Sängerin blieb nur sich querzulegen.

Damals im Staub grober Quader, heute auf nassem Asphalt.
Immer war Völkerwanderung, meistens Gefahr auf den Wegen.

IN THE PROVINCES V

As though brushed by the cart of a fleeing settler,
The dead blackbird lay on the Roman road, in tatters.

One who was always there, always indifferent, the wind
Had hoisted a black sail out of the wings.

And that's how you spotted her from afar, knocked aside,
Your sister pinned now to the earth by the marauding hordes,

Whether Dacians or Huns, Mongol ponies or Vespas—
She had always been a cross distraction from the proximity of her nest.

And that was it. No protracted death agonies.
The poor diva had only to lay herself down

On dusty stone slabs then, or damp asphalt now. People were forever
Migrating, and their roads generally attended by danger.

Nichts ist schlimmer als dieser tödliche Rückweg
Nach einer Schlacht, und der Gedanke daran
Wochen bevor der Feind sich gezeigt hat.
Todfinster ist das Gesicht des Feldherrn,
Die Truppe erschöpft, kein Eilmarsch mehr möglich.
Hinter den Schilden geht schweißnaß, die Füße wund
Der Rest der noch Unverletzten. Im Dauerregen
Sind die Pfade im Schlamm versunken, die Wälder
Ein einziger Hinterhalt, und die Barbaren in Rudeln
Beißen sich Stücke aus unseren Rücken, die Wölfe.
Wer nicht im Nordmeer ertrank, fern der Heimat,
Den schlucken die Sümpfe, weit weg von Rom.
Über Nacht hält Morast die ganze Legion,
Tags sind es morsche Dämme, brüchige Leitern,
Von deren Rand mit gebrochenen Fingern
Der Einzelne abrutscht. Das Land liegt im Nebel
Wie eine Inselgruppe im Meer . . . *Germania Magna*,
Wo die Wälder noch dicht sind, kein Baum
Auf dem Ozean treibt als Galeerenbank
Oder als brennender Schiffsrumpf. Aussichtslos
Ist der Krieg um Provinzen groß wie ein Erdteil,
Um Gebiete, die nicht zu halten sind,
Außer durch neuen Krieg. In den waldigen Tiefen
Verliert der Triumph sich, die lateinische Ordnung.
Und kommst du endlich, um Jahre gealtert, nach Haus,
Steht der Germane in deiner Tür, und es winkt dir
Das strohblonde Kind deiner Frau.

LAMENT OF A LEGIONNAIRE ON GERMANICUS'S CAMPAIGN TO THE ELBE RIVER

There's nothing worse than this deadly retreat
following a battle, except the same retreat in prospect
weeks before . . .
Black as death the expression on the general's face,
the shambling, exhausted troops.
Behind the shields are the remnants of those unhurt,
footsore, running
with sweat. Incessant rain
has softened the tracks, the woods are one long ambush,
and the barbarians in packs, the wolves,
bite pieces out of our rear guard.
Whoever did not drown in the North Sea, far from home,
goes down in the swamps, as remote from the eternal city.
Overnight, morasses detain the whole legion,
by day it's rotten causeways, moldering ladders,
from whose rungs a man slips to his death
with fingers crushed. This land merely punctuates fog
like some archipelago at sea . . . Germania Magna,
where the forests are still integral and dense,
no tree bobs on the sea cut to a bank of oars—
or a blazing hulk. The futility of fighting
over provinces as vast as continents, and territories
that can only be defended by further wars.
In the depths of the forest there is no triumph, and no Latin order.
And when, aged by many years, you finally make it home,
it will be to see the German installed under your lintel,
and waving to you your wife's towheaded offspring.

Nicht wahr, sie machen euch Angst, meine Finger,

So lang und so knochig, zehn krumme verdorrte Äste.

Was wird erzählt? Ich könne mit Links einen Apfel durchbohren?

Nicht nur das, liebe Freunde. Auch ein glotzendes Auge.

Auch den Brief, der mir schmeichelt mit blinzelnden kleinen Worten.

Ich brauch keinen Schlagring, mir genügen die Finger —

Dieselben, mit denen ich Krebse esse und Kleinkinder necke.

Wie man vom Tisch eine Fliege schnippt, die dann kreiselnd

Am Boden verendet, so fahr ich dem Staunenden ins Gesicht.

Was wie ein Streicheln aussieht, eine zärtliche Geste,

Ist mein gefährlichster Schlag. Nicht wahr, das brennt,

Und macht blutige Striemen. Hab ich den Feind erst markiert,

Bin ich ganz sicher, es findet sich einer, der ihn beseitigt für mich.

Ich aber zieh mich zurück, trauernd. Das Schlachten widert mich an.

There, they scare you, don't they, my fingers
Long and bony like ten gnarled and twisted branches.
What is it people say about me? That I can drill through
    an apple with my forefinger?
That's not all, possums. The apple of an eye's even easier.
The letter that seeks to flatter me with little honeyed words.
I don't use a spike or knuckleduster, my bare fingers are enough—
The same as the ones I like to eat crabs and torture children with.
No different than swatting aside a fly, which will go spinning
To the ground, I like to smack some poor unfortunate.
What might look like an affectionate caress
Is my most dangerous blow. There, it burns, doesn't it,
And it leaves a nasty raised welt. Once I've marked the enemy,
I expect someone will come along and get rid of him for me.
I meanwhile withdraw, grieving. Bloodshed upsets me.

CLUB OF ROME

Für Arno Widmann

Tote Carthagos im Rücken, vor den Augen schneeweiß,
Die Alpen, ein Friedhof für Elefanten,
War nicht der Römer ein Überlebender, dem die Zeit
Ostwärts davonlief?

Unterm Fuß Katakomben, in deren tropfenden Gängen
Fanatiker wohnten, Verdammung kochend
Mit dem täglichen Mahl, war die Angst vor Barbaren
Sein letzter Zauber.

Denn Treppen und Vasen glänzten heller aus jedem Riß
Im Marmor. Wie im Bordell die Matratzen,
War der Limes zerschlissen. Aus Waldböden schossen
Feinde wie Pilze.

Schatten wuchsen, von der kälteren Seite des Mondes,
Über verwilderte Gärten. An Sarkophagen
Wurden Schweine gemästet. Im Grundwasser schlierte
Blut aus Latrinen.

Nur die alten Herren, bewundert, intrigierten mit Lust
Um verpachtete Güter. Ihr großes Spiel
War der Wechsel von Lachen und Weinen; ihr Credo —
›Nach uns die Schlammflut‹.

CLUB OF ROME

for Arno Widmann

Deleted Carthages behind them, and sheer ahead of them
Blinding white Alps, elephants' graveyards—
Wasn't the Roman a survivor, from whom time
Fled eastwards?

Underfoot were catacombs in whose dripping tunnels
Dwelt fanatics, stoking the fires of hell to boil
Their once-a-day porridge; fear of the barbarians still
Worked like a charm.

Vases and staircases gleamed more brightly
For every chip in the marble. The threshold creaked
Like the mattresses in the brothels. Enemies sprang up
Like mushrooms in the forests.

Lunar shadows lengthened to cover the rank expanse
Of the gardens. Hogs were fattened
On sarcophagi. The water supply was laced with blood
From the public latrines.

Only a few admirable oldsters went on
Gleefully buying up their neighbors' erstwhile estates. Their speciality
Was the seamless alternation between laughter and tears; their refain,
"Après nous—etcetera."

All die Sitzkissen schwitzen. All die Zierfische japsen
Hinter Panzerglas, wo das Wasser wie von Brausetabletten schäumt
Und die Algen sich Blut zufächeln. Mit zerfressenen Flossen
Ging der Krieg im Aquarium zuende. Der dickliche Guppy träumt.
Vor dem Sofa, verrenkt, liegt ein Strumpfpaar mit Strapsen,
In den letzten Zügen im Kristall die Zigarre. Wie hingegossen
Breiten sich Stoffbahnen aus um die Fenster, knöcheltief, Kelims.
Im ganzen Apartment schmelzen, an den Wänden in goldenen Tiegeln,
Pastose Farben zu etwas, das Rosen ähnelt, Mondgebirgen,
    Phlegmonen, —
Ein Frauenakt hier, dort eine Bibelszene. Pro Glasschrank drei Spiegel
Decken den Rückzug ins Labyrinth. Was da klirrt als *Klimbim*,
Die Fayencen, die Lüster schmeicheln den feisten, kinderlosen
    Bewohnern,
Die auf Kommoden von Photos lächeln, auf Kreuzfahrt, die ewige Crew.
Im Radio liest jemand, sich klösterlich räuspernd, das Decamerone,
Und nur der Afghane, sein Fell eins mit den Teppichfransen, hört zu.
›Wie es war, willst du wissen, *chérie*? Wie mit himmlischen Geigen . . .
Gespielt? War das Stöhnen gespielt? Frag die Fische, sie schweigen.‹

Heaving with throw cushions. All the ornamental fish are yapping

Behind thickened glass, in water effervescing like Alka Seltzer.

Algae fan themselves with fresh blood. Peace returns to the aquarium,

At the expense of a few chewed up fins. The guppy stoutly dreams.

A pair of stockings plus garters is writhing at the foot of the sofa,

A portly cigar, with cummerbund, blows smoke rings from the massy
   ashtray.

Kilims, ankle-deep, unroll clear to the windows, like red carpets.

In golden palettes all over the apartment, glutinous colors

Are melting to the likeness of a rose, moon mountains, phlegmons—

Female nude here, Old Testament scene there. Three mirrors per glass-
   fronted cabinet

To cover your retreat into the labyrinth. Kickshaws on the mantelpiece,

Faience pottery and candelabra flatter the dependably childless denizens,

Smiling from framed photographs on tallboys, cruise snaps, captain and
   crew.

On the wireless someone with a nasty monastic cough is reading *The
   Decameron*,

Though only the Afghan hound, blending in so nicely with the carpet
   tassels, seems to be attending.

"Shall I describe it to you, sweetness? The music of the spheres . . .
   Faked?

I suppose your orgasm was faked, too? Don't take my word for it then,
   ask the fishes."

So teure Pelze sieht man sonst nur auf den Schultern
Der Gangsterbräute vorm Casino. So geschmeidig
Schleicht auf dem Laufsteg nur die androgyne Jugend,
Die Augen funkelnd unterm Blitzlicht. Eine schlanke Katze,
Wie Pisanello sie gemalt hat, mit entzücktem Pinsel
(Das Fell getüpfelt, grannenhaft, ein Goldnes Vließ)
Federt sie schweifend auf und ab. Das Rückgrat
Dosiert die leiseste Bewegung.
                              Millimeter
Vorm Grabenrand den Schwung der Pfoten umzulenken
Geht ohne Hinsehn ab. Dort wird dem Ohr,
Der feinen Nase nichts geboten außer Lärm und Schweiß,
Jenseits des Drahtzauns, wo sich diese Affen tummeln
Mit ihren Kinderwagen zur Besuchszeit. Hechelnd
Verwandelt sie die schlechte Luft der Großstadt
In ein entferntes Air . . . die weißen Schleifen
Im Haar der Mädchen in Gazellenfleisch. Faustgroß,
Ihr schmaler Kopf hält wachsam noch die Stellung,
Wenn sie im Flimmern vor den Toren Moskaus Zebras sieht.
Dann gähnt sie lange, die Gefangne des Zements.

Furs this expensive you normally only find wrapped around the shoulders
Of gangsters' molls outside the casino, movements this slinky
Only on the catwalk from the androgynous models,
Eyes dilating in the flashbulbs. As lean a feline
As Pisanello once painted with ravished brush
(The fur spotted, whiskery, a golden fleece).
She sashays swishing up and back. Her spine measures out
The least movement.
                              To change direction
Millimeters in front of the ditch is something for which
She doesn't even need eyes. There's nothing out there
For the ear or the sensitive nose but the noise and sweat
Beyond the wire fence, where those monkeys congregate
With their baby carriages at visiting time. Her breath
Coming hard, she magics the fetor of the metropolis
Into a charmed ozone . . . the white ribbons
In the girls' hair into strips of gazelle meat. Her fine head,
No bigger than your fist, keeps its alert posture
As she spies zebras in the flickering at the gates of Moscow.
Then she yawns, the prisoner of the cement.

Alles geht weiter, nicht erst seit heute, vor allem der Krieg,
Das Anziehn täglich, das Ausziehn. Der schmerzhaften Nähe
Der beiden Körperhälften, der Ferne von Ich zu Gesicht,
Zu entfliehen hilft nichts. Und getötet, gezeugt,
Wird hier nicht nur aus Armut, zum Zeitvertreib auch.

Doch die Dichter, man weiß es, sind schwierige Leute,
Die nichts mehr stiften. Selbst das Gelächter
Klingt ohne sie schärfer. Es gilt ihnen kaum.

Nachdem er das Böse verherrlicht hatte und die Gewalt,
Sechs Gesänge lang, kehrte er um, Lautréamont der Skorpion.
Sein Epos vom Guten blieb ein frommer Entwurf.

Baudelaire, mit stumpfer Klinge zum Selbstmord bereit
Beim Erscheinen der ersten großformatigen Zeitung,
Glaubte das Ende der Dichtung nah, nicht zum letzten Mal.

Everything continues much as before, especially the war,
But also the daily dressing and undressing. The left and right half
Of the body remained conjoined, and there's still that chasm
Between reflection and self. And people kill and breed
Not just out of desperation, but to pass the time.

Poets, so they tell us, are awkward customers
Not up to much. Even laughter has a keener, full-throated edge
When they're not around. They're not very amusing.

After hymning evil and violence in six long cycles,
Lautréamont the scorpion wheeled around.
His magnum opus on good remained a pious sketch.

Baudelaire, prepared to saw through his throat with a blunt knife
When the first broadsheet newspaper was printed,
Thought, not for the last time, the end of poetry was nigh.

ASCHE ZUM FRÜHSTÜCK

DREIZEHN FANTASIESTÜCKE

Und dann kommt der heitere Teil vom Sterben. Versöhnt
Mit dem Tag der Geschäfte verspricht und Verträge bricht,
Drehst du dich früh aus dem Spiegel. Dein gebrauchtes Gesicht,
Scharf rasiert, das dem Quengeln von innen höhnt,
Gehört dem Empfangschef, der die Verhandlungen führt.
Hinterm Jochbein verschanzt, hinter funkelnder Brille —
Hat seine Leichenblässe dich nicht manchmal gerührt?
Sicher, man kennt sich. Das heißt, ohne Promille
Tritt keiner dem andern zu nah (und auch das besser selten).
Denn vor der schmierigen Wand, konzentriert auf das Gelbe
Im Porzellan, ist man wieder der Andre, wieder derselbe,
Dem im Moment der Entleerung die Klassiker gelten.
›Alles fließt.‹ ›Hör auf in den Eingeweiden zu wühlen.‹
›Lebe verborgen.‹ ›Erkenne dich selbst.‹
Doch bevor du hier fortgehst, vergiß nicht zu spülen.

THIRTEEN FANTASIES

And then comes the fun part of dying. Braced
For the deal-making, contract-breaking day,
You wheel sharply away from the mirror.

                        Your lived-in face,
Closely shaved, that mocks the grizzling inside of you,
Is at the service of the CEO who's leading the negotiations.
Somewhere behind your collarbone, or the glitter of your spectacles
—Hasn't his ghostly pallor even, on occasion, moved you?
You know each other, don't you. Without a drink, of course,
You're careful not to get too close (and even with,
You try to avoid it). Because face-to-face with the scribbles on the walls,
Attending to the dribble of yellow into china,
You are once again the Other, the one whose mind,
At the moment of voiding, is enviably stocked with the Classics.
"All things flow." "Stop digging around in the intestines."
"Live guardedly." "Know thyself."
And, less Classical, remember to flush afterward.

(VON DEN DOPPELGÄNGERN)

Doch dann wird es Zeit, sich den Rücken zu kehren. Die Tür
Läßt den Affenkäfig vergessen, das Namensschild Darwins Coup
Den gespreizten Daumen zu deuten, den Pelz unterm Hemd. Und wofür
Sind Schuhe und Hausecken da, wenn nicht, um ihn abzuschütteln,
Den Wächter am Stammbaum, der die Sprünge vom Sie zum Du
Pantomimisch begleitet.
               Vom Totschlag mit Knütteln
Lenken ihn Türschlösser ab, Geldbörsen, Knöpfe, Telephonhörer —
Alles was griffbereit ist, woran sich fummeln läßt rund um die Uhr,
Weil die Finger, verdoppelt, sich kreuzen. Unrast, der große Zerstörer,
Macht aus dem Läusesammeln die tausend Verrichtungen täglich.
Zwischen Imbiß und Beischlaf wie oft, fern der Oldoway-Schlucht,
Zeigt der haarige Kerl sich, humpelnd auf Fäusten, und scheitert kläglich,
Wo die Leiter schief steht, der Lift klemmt, beim schönsten Höhenflug.
(Soviel zum *Ursprung der Arten*, zum *Unbehagen in der Kultur*.)

(ON DOPPELGÄNGERS)

But then the time comes when we must turn our back on ourselves.
The door closes off our memories of the monkey cage, the nameplate
    blots out
Darwin's coup in interpreting the thumb, the chest rug under the shirt.
And what else are shoes and house corners for, if not to shake him off,
That guardian of our family tree, lending his mimed accompaniment to
    our leap
From *"Oy"* to "Citizen."

                             He is distracted from bludgeoning us to death
By Yale locks, wallets, buttons, telephone keyboards,
Anything that's to hand for you to fiddle with round the clock.
Because the fingers, doubled, tie themselves in knots. Restlessness, the
    ruin of our species,
Has adapted louse-hunting into a thousand delicate negotiations per
    diem.
Between snack bar and coitus, how often, miles from the Olduvai Gorge,
The hairy geezer puts in an appearance, hobbling along on the backs of
    his hands,
Failing abjectly as he reaches for the stars, because of a crooked ladder or
    a jammed elevator.
(So much for *The Origin of Species* or *Civilization and Its Discontents*.)

(DIS MANIBUS)

Abgeräumt das Lokal, verlassen von den guten, den bösen Geistern
Die Caféhaustische, die Leseecken, die blitzenden Theken.
Jetzt sind sie allein, Infizierte, mit ihren Meistern,
Die von der Sprechzeit nichts wissen in den Bibliotheken.

Und wie Fliegen im Doppelfenster (weder drinnen noch draußen)
Die grannigen Beine reiben, ermattet vom nahen Vakuum,
Holt sie der Juckreiz ein. Sie kratzen sich in den trostlosen Pausen,
Wenn die Bücher zusammenrücken und klar wird, sie bleiben stumm.

(DIS MANIBUS)

The place is tidied away, abandoned by its bright sparks and ill spirits,
The café tables, reading nooks, and gleaming bars.
Now they are all alone, the infected ones, with their masters,
Ignorant of the visiting hours in libraries.

And just as flies in double glazing (neither in nor out)
Chafe their furry legs, flagging in the near vacuum,
They are overtaken by their itch. They scratch themselves in those
    dismal intervals
When the books close ranks and it transpires they don't speak.

(VON DER EINS IN DER MENGE)

Du aber warst bald erkannt in deinen scharf gebügelten Hosen.
Doch es macht dir nichts aus, wie es scheint, pfeifend weiter zu gehn.
Ein Gefühl von Preisschild im Nacken, was? Unter der Zunge
Den Geschmack von Leitungswasser und von Konservendosen.
Streng als Eins lebst du hin. Gewöhnt an die Ordnung der Zehn . . .
Rechnend nur mit den zählbaren Dingen. Egal, wie verschlungen
Laokoon war, — du bist dieser vorwärts rückende Strich
In beengten Straßen, das Komma, fehlplaziert, eines fleißigen Setzers,
Dem die Stadt in Gedrucktes zerfällt, in Tabellen und Spalten.
Und die zwei mal zwölf Stunden, die Kolumnen elektrischen Lichts,
Sind Versprechen genug. Offnen Munds lernst du schätzen,
Was die vielen Gesichter der Null niemals halten.

(OF THE ONE IN THE CROWD)

You, with your knife-edged trouser-creases, were soon spotted,
But it seemed to make no odds to you, and you went whistling on.
Feel the price tag at the back of your neck? Annoying, isn't it?
On your tongue the taste of tap water and canned food.
You live as One. Used to the system of decimals,
Only relying on things that stack up. Never mind Laocoön in his toils—
You are the vertical line moving ahead through narrow streets,
The misplaced comma of an over-eager typesetter,
To whom the city falls into printed matter, columns, and tables.
And the twice twelve hours, the rota of electric light,
Is promise enough. Openmouthed, you learn to esteem
What the many zero faces never grasp.

(VON DER INNEREN UNRUH)

Und wie ist es mit dir? Schon mal ans Aufhörn gedacht?
Das Hirn, kaum allein, schon verwahrlost, spielt mit jedem Gedanken,
Wenn er nur groß genug ist und in Riesenschritten zum Ende führt.
Lieber als Erdnüsse knacken, sprich die Minuten, ist ihm die Schlacht
Gegen den übrigen Körper, den traurigen Rest. In die zitternden
    Flanken
Stößt es gern mit brutaler Neugier. Ein Reporter, der ungerührt
Die Zerstörung studiert, als sei sie *sein* Werk, nicht das einer dritten
    Kraft.
Die zu verleugnen, ist jedes Mittel ihm recht.
                         Es begrüßt die Gewalt,
Die von Dingen ausgeht und Worten. Dank der Verletzungen, der
    Gravuren,
Kann es sich trösten, früh übergangen zu sein und demnächst
    abgeschafft.
So wird der Aschenbecher, schwer auf dem Tisch, zum willkommenen
    Halt
Am Abhang der Tage. Die innere Unruh zum Schutz vor den Uhren.

(OF INNER UNREST)

And what about you? Ever think of calling the whole thing off?
The brain, no sooner alone, already neglected, entertains every thought
So long as it's big enough, and cuts to the chase.
Sooner than crack peanuts, or minutes, it would take on
The rest of the body, the sorry remainder. With brutal curiosity,
It likes to batter the trembling flanks. A reporter,
Coolly studying destruction, as if it were its own handicraft,
Not someone else's. Anything to deny that.
                                        It acclaims the violence
That goes out from things and words. Injuries and scratch marks
Console it, reconcile it to its obscurity and obsolescence.
So the ashtray, resting on the table, quickly becomes a welcome
Support on slippery days. Inner unrest as protection against clocks.

(VON DER ÖFFENTLICHEN HAND)

Nein, was nie liegen bleibt, ist Geld. Blinkt auf der Straße,
Kopf oder Zahl, ein rundes Stück Metall, macht man den Diener.
Denn jede Münze scheint, wie durch den Schlitz gefallen, deplaziert,
Dort wo man hinspuckt und sich ausweicht. Spürt die Hundenase
Im Bodensatz nicht jeden Heller auf? Und setzt man, ganz Schlawiner,
Den Fuß nicht auf das Fundstück, pfeifend, als sei nichts passiert?
Warum, wenn der Triumph nur pfennigweise kommt, und niemals nie
Sind unter all den Groschen Silbertaler, Golddukaten?
Denn meistens apportiert man nur den Hosenknopf und läßt
Mit roten Hängeohren seine Beute los, ruft jemand ›*Iih!*‹.
Geld zieht den Blick an, magisch, macht den Arm zum Automaten,
An dem der Greifer zuckt, und was er packt, das hält er fest.
In aller Gier rührt tief im Müll — die öffentliche Hand,
Der es egal ist, was sie dort zu fassen kriegt. Statt einer schlanken,
Frisierten Göttin im Profil schiebt sich ein Kanzler in die Schwielen.
Wär dir ein Kaiser lieber, ein Torero? Schmeicheln Yen und Krüger-
    Rand
Der Haut wie Kauri-Muscheln? Und gehört nicht alles Geld den
    Banken?
Ach, daß man immer wieder Kleinkind ist, in den Fäkalien spielend.

(ON CURRENCY)

One thing never left lying around is money. Whenever you see anything
Round and glinting on the pavement, heads or tails, you stoop to
    conquer.
Because every coin seems out of place, where normally people spit
Or tread. Doesn't the dog's nose sniff every penny on the floor?
And don't you cannily set your foot on the find, and whistle innocence?
Why are these triumphs penny-wise, and never silver talers or gold
    ducats,
And often enough you come up with a trouser button, and blushing
    drop your treasure
While someone jeers! Money draws your eye, magically,
Turns your arm to a mechanical claw that grasps what it holds.
In all that greed, deep in the junk, is self-help.
No slim, coiffed goddess, but a feisty Chancellor between your fingers.
Would you rather an emperor, or a torero? Do yen and Krugerrands
Flatter the skin like cowrie shells? Isn't all money the property
In any case of the bank? Oh, to be a child again, grubbing in real feces.

*   *   *

Und warum, fragt man sich (und *Warum* ist die kindlichste Frage)
Bin ich ausgesetzt dem Parcours, diesem Lauf auf verkauftem Boden,
Wo die tote Taube zum Fußball wird, den der Schwächlichste kickt.

Still gezeugt von Verliebten, wer weiß, auf der nächstbesten Trage
Beiseitegeschafft nach dem Herzinfarkt, mit erkalteten Hoden.
Einer, der weiß, wann ein Wort nicht mehr wirkt. Der verschlossen
   nickt,

Weil auch Lächeln trügt, Scham, und der Mund gern den Rachen deckt.
Sind die tragischsten Rollen nicht stumm? Und wie viele Szenen
Bleiben unbezeugt, eh der Lappen flink übers Wachstuch streicht.

Menschen ändern sich, Städte, doch nicht am Nabel der Leberfleck.
Und wehe, du beugst dich nicht, eine Kußhand hier, dort ein Dehnen
Akrobatischer Glieder, — diesem Leben, so unnütz, so reich.

*   *   *

And why, you ask yourself (why being the most childish of questions),
Why am I involved in this rat race on bartered ground,
Where these weaklings are kicking around a dead pigeon.

Silently bred out of love, only to be, who knows, hauled onto the nearest
    stretcher
After the cardiac event, with rapidly cooling testicles.
Someone who knows when a word has run out. Who nods silently,

Because a smile or blush is too much of a deception, and the mouth
    prefers to keep the throat covered anyway.
Aren't tragic parts generally mute? And how many scenes there are
That go unwitnessed, before the duster wipes the coffin down.

People change, cities change, but the mole beside your navel stays put.
And woe if you don't perform your reverences, kissing a hand here,
    inclining
Your supple torso there—to this life, so useless, so rich.

Wie die Ufer versteinern . . . Nur er schaut aufs Meer hin wie immer.
›Dieses winzige Zweibein, wer ist das?‹, fragen sich stumm die Gerüste
Am neusten Büroturm, die skelettsteifen Kräne. ›Absolut spinnert‹,
Gähnt ein Erdloch und stinkt.

                     Aus dem Schiffbruch kein Zimmer,
Vom Kinderbett keine Planke blieb übrig. ›Nicht, daß ich wüßte‹,
Schweigt ein Sperrzaun, befragt, ob der Mensch ihn an etwas erinnert.
Doch er kann es nicht lassen. Tief im Landesinnern gestrandet,
Sind die Dächer der Vorstadt sein Horizont, den er absucht. Wonach?
Aus den Segeln wurde die Leinwand der Kinos. Was draußen brandet,
Ist nur der Autoverkehr. Kein Mast, der ihm nicht droht ›Dich leg ich
    flach‹.
›Verpiß dich!‹ schallt es von jedem Friedhof, den die Bulldozer räumen,
Weil die Liegezeit um ist, verjährt sind die Abos für morsche Gebeine.
Allerorts treibt ein Blaulicht durch Straßen, ohrenbetäubend — — tatüü,
    tatüü!
Nur er grast den Beton ab, Sammler von Strandgut, kommt nie ins
    Reine,
Wenn am Freitag zum Beispiel, auf hohem Absatz, genug zum Träumen,
Ein Chanson mit den Hüften schwenkt: ›*La mort vient et je suis nu . . . .*‹.

These petrifying coasts . . . Only he gazes out to sea, as ever.

"Who is that biped anyway?" the scaffolding poles on the new office block,

The skeleton-stiff cranes, inquire silently of one another. "Fucking bonkers,"

Yawns a malodorous hole in the ground.

                           Not one room, not one plank of his cot

That survived the shipwreck. "Nothing I can put a name to," silently replies

A security fence, when asked whether the fellow reminded him of anything.

But he can't let it go. Stranded somewhere in the interior,

The suburban roofs are the horizon that he scans. What for?

His sails are now the screens of multiplex cinemas. The foaming waves

Are traffic noise. No mast that doesn't say: "I'll flatten you."

"And you can piss off!" he hears from the graveyard that the bulldozers

Are clearing, because time's up for moldy bones, their concession's run its term.

Everywhere the flashing lights and sirens of the emergency services—

That deafening *da-du*, *da-du*—only he, beachcomber, keeps grazing the concrete,

Fails to get it when, on a Friday night for instance, on high heels, the stuff of dreams,

A chanson teeters past, hips swinging: "*La mort vient et je suis nu . . .*"

(VON DEN TAGESZEITUNGEN)

Ich habe Asche gegessen zum Frühstück, den schwarzen
Staub, der aus Zeitungen fällt, aus den druckfrischen Spalten,
Wo ein Putsch keine Flecken macht und der Wirbelsturm steht.
Und es schien mir, als schmatzten sie, die parlierenden Parzen,

Wenn im Sportteil der Krieg begann, dem der Aktienkurs traut.
Ich habe Asche gegessen zum Frühstück. Meine Tagesdiät.
Und von Clio, wie immer, kein Sterbenswort . . . Da, beim Falten,
Lief das Rascheln der Seiten als Schauer mir über die Haut.

(ON THE DAILY NEWSPAPERS)

I have breakfasted on ashes, the black
Dust that comes off newspapers, from the freshly printed columns.
When a coup makes no stain, and a tornado sticks to half a page.
And it seemed to me as though the Fates licked their lips

When war broke out in the sports section, reflected in the falling Dow.
I have breakfasted on ashes. My daily bread.
And Clio, as ever, keeps mum . . . There, just as I folded them up,
The rustling pages sent a shiver down my spine.

(VON DEN REDEN IM SCHLAF)

Der Schaden ist angerichtet. Jetzt kannst du sehen.

Was ein Leben zusammenhält, ist das Loch im Kalender.

Kein Apoll, jeder Typ an der Ecke sagt dir, du mußt es ändern.

Denn geweint wird hier viel. Doch nur einmal lag in den Wehen

Wegen dir eine Frau, und nur einmal war um dich ein Zittern,

Das die Mauern durchdrang. He, ihr Lauscher, so fing es an.

Wenn die Fichten vom Regen triefen, am Christbaum Lametta flittert,

Werden die Knie weich, jedes Jahr wieder.

                       Kein schmerzender Zahn

Sticht den Druck toter Tage aus, dieses Heimweh nach Ungelebtem.

Du blinzelst? Der Schaden ist angerichtet. Was man hier sieht,

Ist so anders als alles, was den vom Lutschen verklebten

Daumen verheißungsvoll machte. Wonach der Säugling schrie.

Jedes Tischtuch zeigt, der Fleck, um den gestern schon Fliegen
    spazierten,

Daß die Stunde wie Ware verderblich ist, wieder kein Wunder geschah.

Wo ein Datum ist, hat der Körper das Nachsehn, der Letztplazierte.

Je weiter er geht, umso tiefer versinkt er, zuletzt über beide Ohren.

Und wer weiß, ob es Scham ist, vielleicht überlebt nur das *Blablabla*.

Der Schaden ist angerichtet. Die Bande, wo ist sie, der Liquidatoren?

(ON TALKING IN ONE'S SLEEP)

The damage has been done. Now you'll see.

What holds a life together is a window in a calendar.

Even the man from Omaha—no Apollo he—will tell you

You must change it. A lot of crying goes on here.

But only once did a woman experience birth pangs over you,

And only once were you the subject of a convulsion

That went through the walls. Hey, snoopers, that's how it began.

When the evergreen drips with rain, and Christmas trees sparkle with
tinsel

The knees go weak, reliably, year on year.

                                No toothache or neuralgia

Can suppress the pressure of dead days, that longing for an unlived life.

Are you sniveling? The damage has been done. What you see here

Is utterly different from whatever it was that made your thumb,

Sticky from sucking, so distinctly promising. Worth bawling for.

The tablecloth, the stain the flies investigated only yesterday,

Will testify that the hour is endlessly perishable, that the miracle has not
taken place.

Where there is a date, the body, bringing up the rear, had better look to
itself.

And the further it goes, the deeper it sinks, ultimately in over both ears.

And who knows whether it's shame, maybe what will survive of us is

Blah . . .

The damage has been done. Someone, call in the receiver!

(VON DER SCHÖNHEIT DER HÄMATOME)

Blut stillt sich selbst. Was da schmerzt, bleibt Geheimnis der Haut,
Die den Einsiedler deckt, bis zuletzt, und nach Stößen begehrt.
Knochensatt knirscht die Erde. Aus jeder Einsamkeit sickert Zeit.
Deshalb die Spielchen zu zweit . . . Wenn am Schenkel ein Veilchen
    blaut,

Ruft Verdacht gern den Teufel zurück, den altersschwachen Gefährten.
Dabei blüht sie nur Tage, etruskisch schön, unter Nylons und Kleid,
Die gebügelte Orchis. Aus der Rüsche, blutunterlaufen, der Raute,
Wird ein gelbgrüner Schmierfleck, der höhnt ›Sieh doch hin, du wirst
    alt‹.

Und schon ist sie wertlos, die blaue Mauritius dort überm Knie,
Die holzige Stelle.
                War der Mensch nicht das Tier, das Kaugummi kaute,
Als es Eden verließ und zur Mondlandung aufbrach, von Liebe und π
Überrascht wie im Sommer der Fuß, wenn er kleben bleibt am Asphalt.

(ON THE BEAUTY OF HEMATOMAS)

Blood allays itself. Pain remains the skin's secret,
Mapping the intruder till the end, and asking for soft knocks.
The bone-stuffed earth crunches underfoot. Time leaks out of solitude,
Hence our little twosomes . . . When a violet flowers on the thigh,

Suspicion is apt to fall on the devil, the senile old companion.
But it only blooms for days, Etruscan and beautiful, under stockings and
    dress,
A pressed orchid. A blood-frilled quadrilateral
Becomes a chartreuse smear that mocks: "Look, you're getting on."

And soon enough it's lost all value, the blue Mauritius above the knee.
The duff spot.
           Was man not the animal who chewed gum
When he left Eden and blasted off for the moon, bemused by love and π
Like your foot when it sticks, in summer, to the asphalt.

(VON DEN FALSCHEN BEWEGUNGEN)

Was sind das für Tage, die als springende Fohlen beginnen,
Und die Nacht ist der Igel, der am Straßenrand seine Blutspur zieht?
Wer morgens aufbrach, das Fürchten zu lernen, federleicht auf dem Kies,
Steht am Ende des Rundgangs, Beine breit, über glucksenden
    Regenrinnen.
Dann schwimmt vorbei, was Andromeda an die Warenhäuser verriet,
Vermischt mit Sekreten, der Brühe, die aus gewissen Kliniken fließt.
Unmöglich, das Glückskind zu bleiben.
                         Wer einmal sah, wie der Hieb
Kalt in den Rücken traf, wie die Wespe den offenen Kindermund fand,
Hält sich raus aus dem Feilschen, aus ›Vater unser . . . ‹ und ›Selig
    sind . . . ‹.
›Zu spät!‹ schreit Herr Schadenfroh beim Anblick der blutenden Hand.
Drei Ecken weiter, am Taxistand, tönt es schon ›Haltet den Dieb!‹.
Mit jedem Vollmond feiert Ohnmacht ein Jubiläum.
                         Fledermausblind
Bahnt sich das Unheil, bürokratisch, seinen Weg durch die Menge.
Mit einer Gräte im Hals endet, was als Diner in fünf Gängen begann.
Kein ›O weh!‹ nimmt die Zentnerlast vom gequetschten Zeh,
Wenn der *Pas de deux* zum Gewichtheben wurde. Im größten Gedränge
Macht noch die schlichteste Botschaft den Passanten als Reißer an,
Wie auf dem nassen Filmplakat der verschwommene Titel
    ›Theo-di-zee‹.

(ON FALSE MOVEMENTS)

What days are these, that begin like frolicsome foals, and by night
Are hedgehogs schlepping their bloody bulk along the side of the road?
Whoever set off bright and early to learn about fear, crisply crunching on
    the gravel,
By the end of the tour stands spraddle-legged over gurgling gutters,
Full of Andromeda's gift of department stores,
Mixed with secretions and the effluent from certain clinics.
Impossible to remain Fortunatus.
                             Whoever once saw the stab in the back,
Or the wasp find the child's open mouth, will have nothing to do
With the wheedling and cringing, the "Our Father," and "Blessed are . . ."
"Too late!" cries Mr. Sadist as he sees the bloodied hand—
Three streets along, at the taxi stand, there's the next cry of "Stop, thief!"
Every full moon is an anniversary of helplessness.
                             Purblind, fussy
Catastrophe clears a path through the crowd ("Gangway!").
A five-course dinner ends with a fish bone lodged in the throat . . .
No amount of "Oh woe!" will lift the dumbbell off the crushed toe,
Once the pas de deux turned into a weight-lifting contest.
In the crush, the plainest news assails the passerby
Like the sodden film poster with its blurred "The-o-di-cy."

(VOM HIER UND JETZT)

Was, wenn der Blick immer früher zurückkehrt, das brave Tier,
Dem nichts Menschliches fremd ist? Alles Neue macht es nur müde.
Überschaubar geworden, illustriert, fällt es leicht durch den Schlitz
Der entzündeten Lider: dies protzige Jetzt, dies verstiegene Hier.
Was immer piano beginnt, wie auf Mäusepfötchen und als Etüde,
Dröhnt aus sämtlichen Boxen zuletzt. Im Fortissimo schwitzt
Die versammelte Meute, laut kreischend ›*Pan ist tot! Pan ist tot!*‹.
Nicht mal im Unbewußten steht Zeit so still, daß man unbeschwert
Atmend verweilen könnte. Im Nu sind die Augenblicke verpatzt,
Da der Ton noch schwebt, das Gesicht. Wiederholung droht
Jeder primären Regung. Mit einem Bleistift zur Schädelnaht quer
Kritzelt steif eine Hand den erlernten Namen. Gott, wie das kratzt.

(ON THE HERE AND NOW)

What if your glance finds it ever harder to be away, the nice pet
That found nothing human alien to itself? Now novelty just tires it out.
Manageable, and with helpful illustrations, it falls easily through the slit
Of your inflamed lids: that pompous now and jumped-up here.
What begins as piano, tiptoeing like a mouse, an étude,
Ends up as stadium rock. The assembled rabble
Sweats it out in fortissimo, screaming, "Pan is dead! Pan is dead!"
Not even in the unconscious does time stand so still that you can stop
And catch your breath. Each instant is instantly ended.
With the note still held, or the expression. Repetition menaces
Any primary impulse. Holding a pencil perpendicular to your skull,
A hand scratches the name it's learned. God, it tickles.

Von meiner weitesten Reise zurück, anderntags
Wird mir klar, ich verstehe vom Reisen nichts.
Im Flugzeug eingesperrt, stundenlang unbeweglich,
Unter mir Wolken, die aussehn wie Wüsten,
Wüsten, die aussehn wie Meere, und Meere,
Den Schneewehen gleich, durch die man streift
Beim Erwachen aus der Narkose, sehe ich ein,
Was es heißt, über die Längengrade zu irren.

Dem Körper ist Zeit gestohlen, den Augen Ruhe.
Das genaue Wort verliert seinen Ort. Der Schwindel
Fliegt auf mit dem Tausch von Jenseits und Hier
In verschiedenen Religionen, mehreren Sprachen.
Überall sind die Rollfelder gleich grau und gleich
Hell die Krankenzimmer. Dort im Transitraum,
Wo Leerzeit umsonst bei Bewußtsein hält,
Wird ein Sprichwort wahr aus den Bars von Atlantis.

Reisen ist ein Vorgeschmack auf die Hölle.

The day after getting back from my longest journey,
I realize I had this traveling business badly wrong.
Penned in an airplane, immobilized for hours on end,
Over clouds that bear the appearance of deserts,
Deserts that bear the appearance of seas, and seas
That are like the blizzards you struggle through,
On your way out of your Halcion-induced stupor,
I see what it means to stumble over the dateline.

The body is robbed of time, and the eyes of rest.
The carefully chosen word loses its locus.
Giddily you juggle the here and the hereinafter,
Keeping several languages and religions up in the air.
But runways are the same gray everywhere, and hospital rooms
The same bright. There in the transit lounge,
Where downtime remains conscious to no end.
The proverb from the bars of Atlantis swims into ken:

Travel is a foretaste of Hell.

Für Christian Döring

I

TAUENTZIENSTRAßE)

Ach, kein Liedchen wirbelt mehr durch diese Straße.
Und der Fahrtwind, der vorbeischaut, flirtet mit den Kanten
Dekorierter Stahlvitrinen, drei vier Stockwerk hoch und voller Waren.
Die hier leben, eilig und in kleinen Raten, sind Passanten.

Kehrmaschinen sorgen nachts für reibungslose Flächen.
Überm Glanz von Eislaufbahnen streuen Leuchtreklamen
Wie Gerüchte Namen aus, von denen es im Telephonbuch wimmelt.
Früh im Schlußverkauf gibt man die letzten bürgerlichen Dramen.

Eine Kirche steht hier, die erinnert streng an Bunker,
Seit ihr Turm, ein abgebrochner Flaschenhals, plombiert ist
Mit demselben Baustoff der im Parkhaus höllisch von Motoren dröhnt.
Taucht ein Lächeln aus dem U-Bahn-Schacht, stößt es auf Maniriertes.

Stecken Zähne im Asphalt, sind sie von Fahrradboten,
Die beim Slalom stürzten oder Fensterputzern, vom Gerüst gefallen.
Grün der Mittelstreifen wird zum Sprungtuch. Durch den Stoßverkehr
Blitzt ein Glücksrad für die einen, wo die andern Bußgeld zahlen.

Wieviel Krimskrams trägt man in den Taschen
Mit sich fort von hier, und wieviel bleibt an Ort und Stelle
Für die junge Archäologin, die im Schutt der legendären Städte kniet,
In der Hand den weichen Pinsel, dieses Echo jeder Maurerkelle.

BERLIN ROUNDS

For Christian Döring

I

TAUENTZIENSTRASSE)

Here no more little songs go skipping down the street,
And the breeze, blowing by, cuts itself on the edges
Of glass and steel emporia, four stories high and stuffed with goods.
Those who live here do so hurriedly and at their peril.

At night, street-sweeping machines produce the requisite sheerness of
    surface.
Above the sheen of ice-skating rinks, neon signs spread—
Rumorlike—the names the phone book is crawling with.
The last bourgeois dramas pop up in the mid-season sales.

There's a church here, somewhat reminiscent of a bunker,
Since its snapped-off tower, a broken bottleneck, has been plugged
With the same stuff as provides the echoes in multistory parking garages.
If a smile emerges from the subway, it will encounter something
    Mannerist.

If there are teeth in the asphalt, they will be those of dispatch riders
Taking a tumble, or window cleaners plunged from their scaffolding.
The green traffic island serves as a trampoline. In the rush-hour traffic,
Some spy fortune's wheel, while others merely cop a fine.

However much junk you cram in your pockets to take with you
When you go, enough will still remain in situ for the young lady
    archaeologist,
Kneeling in the ruins of fabled cities, in her hand a camel-hair brush—
Distant, degenerate descendant of the mason's trowel.

II

Hier haben die Panzer gewendet,
Und Machorkarauch stieg aus dem plumpen Turm.
Wo kein Gleis mehr, kein Reichsbahnzug endet,
Legte sich der *Mongolensturm.*
Griechenland Expreß. Abfahrt der Schönen und Reichen
In verhängten Coupés, südwärts, in Polster gelehnt.
Ein Russe stand an der letzten der Weichen
Und sammelte Uhren ein, Goldschmuck, den Siegeszehnt.
An den Kreuzungen las man kyrillisch. Den Weg
Durch die Trümmeralleen zeigten Dachbalken an.
Den Roten Stern zu belächeln, kein Sakrileg
Wäre schlimmer gewesen. Verworfen der Plan,
Berlin, das Räubernest, zu schleifen wie Karthago,
Im Staub von Brandenburg ein Großstadtschatten.
Doch Gulasch dämpfte bald, Kosakentanz das Largo,
Wenn auch Frau Krause nichts zu lachen hatte.

II

ANHALTER BAHNHOF)

This is where the tanks about-faced
And papyrossa or peace-pipe smoke fumed from their stumpy turrets.
No longer end of the line for any Reichsbahn train,
The Mongol hordes here hit the buffer.
Hellas-Express. The departure of the rich and beautiful,
Cushioned in their private compartments, for the warm south.
A Russian stood as point man,
Collecting watches, jewelry, the victor's tithe.
The rail crossings were marked in Cyrillic. Charred roof beams
Pointed the way through avenues of ruins.
To smirk at the red star would have been
The gravest sacrilege. They let it go, the idea
Of razing Berlin, that nest of vipers, like Carthage,
Leaving the shadow of a metropolis in the Brandenburg sand.
Then goulash steamed and Cossacks danced,
Even if old mother Krause had nothing to laugh about.

III

AM FRIEDRICHSHAIN)

Nein, von Begrüßung konnte keine Rede sein,
Sieht man die Einschußlöcher Haus für Haus.
Es waren Trommelfeuer, keine Salven
Damals am Friedrichshain.

Und vom Verbrüdern war das alles weit entfernt.
Wer im MG-Nest saß, der schoß heraus.
Kann sein, im Park die Hunde und die Malven
Haben dazugelernt.

Die weißen Fahnen zog ein strenger Winter ein.
Verbandszeug brauchte man und Bettuch auch.
Daß in den Kellern keine Bitten halfen,
Ahnt man am Friedrichshain.

III

FRIEDRICHSHAIN)

No, that was no welcome—
Look at the bullet holes in home after home.
Those were volleys, not salvos,
Back then in Friedrichshain.

There wasn't much fraternization.
Anyone in a machine-gun emplacement fired for what he was worth.
Maybe the dogs and haws in the park
Picked up a trick or two.

The white flags were taken down by a cold winter.
Sheets and bandages were needed.
That pleas went unheeded in the cellars
Is something you can sense, in Friedrichshain.

IV

POTSDAMER PLATZ)

Um und um wird die Erde gewühlt für die Hauptstadt *in spe*.
Der nächtlichen Menschenleere gehn Raupen vorweg.
Germania im Bunker, auf preußischem Kanapee,
Von Baggern im Schlaf gestört, wälzt die Hüften im Dreck.

Downtown Berlin hilft der Diva den Gürtel zu lösen.
Und schmachtend macht sie, Walküre, die Schenkel breit.
Das Gehirn, in den hellsten Momenten, den bitterbösen,
Wittert etwas, das nach Zerstörung schreit.

IV

POTSDAMER PLATZ)

They're churning up the ground for the capital city *in spe.*
Earthmovers go in in advance of the nocturnal desolation.
Germania in her bunker, stretched out on her Prussian chaise longue,
Is disturbed in her sleep, and rolls over in the dirt.

It takes *Downtown Berlin* to help the diva loosen up.
Then, panting for it, the great Valkyrie spreads her thighs.
The brain, in its lucid moments of bitterness,
Sniffs something that cries out for destruction.

V

EPILOG)

Was geschieht hier, fragt man, und erkennt nichts wieder,
Schultern eingezogen unter Kränen. War man nicht ein Riese,
Dem die Stadt gehorchte? Plätze schrumpften auf ihr Spielzeugmaß,
Stieg man aus der Erde. *Ein* ›Hatschi!‹ riß ganze Wohnblocks nieder.

Eben war da noch ein Brachfeld, Sand und etwas abgebrannte Wiese,
Die im Stadtplan fehlten. Daß dort Goyas Koloß saß,
Wartend auf die Wiederkehr der Steppe, glaubt dir keiner mehr.
Einmal eingenickt, und alles hinterrücks war parallel versetzt.

Aus dem preußisch blauen Nachmittag in vier Sektoren, zwei Versionen,
War die Stunde grauen Dunsts geworden, wenn im Kreisverkehr
Hinz und Kunz sich überholen. Zappelnd hängt im Straßennetz
Bald die Hälfte der Bevölkerung. Ihr Motto ›*Schneller Wohnen!*‹

Zeigt den Alten, wo es langgeht. Bis auf Grazie, gibts hier vielzuvieles,
Das den Eilschritt nahelegt, den Tunnelblick. Genügt nicht ein Magnet,
Zum Türeöffnen, seit Apartments als Zementbrei aus den Mischern
  quellen?
Einestags entdeckt man, hoch an Glasfassaden festgeschraubt, Reptile,

Die neutralen Augs den Kehraus überwachen. — Daß ihm nichts
  entgeht.
Nur Gewohnheit, dieser Arbeitslose, kehrt zurück an taube Stellen.

V

EPILOGUE)

What's going on here, you ask, nothing looks familiar
As you hunch under cranes. Didn't you use to be a giant
And have the place at your feet? Squares shrank to Lilliputian scale
When you surfaced. One "Atchoo!" brought down whole apartment
    blocks.

This used to be waste ground, sand, and a bit of scorched grass,
Not marked on the map. Now no one believes you when you say
Goya's colossus used to sit here, waiting for it to revert to steppe.
You dropped your guard, and everything was suddenly knocked down.

The Prussian blue afternoon—four sectors, two versions—
Has turned into an hour of gray exhaust, as Tom, Dick, and Harry
Crawl past each other in the rush. Half the population
Is stuck in traffic, their watchword: "Faster living!"

Show the ancients the score. Not too much sign of the Graces
But lockstep and tunnel vision aplenty. Who needs a key for the door,
The way prefab apartments squelch out of cement mixers?
One day your eye lights on reptiles battened to the glass façades—

Unblinking, impassive—supervising the evictions.
It's only habit, downsized, that keeps returning to its dead haunts.

Täglich weht ein leichter Wind hier durchs Gedächtnis.
    Schleift die Eigenschaften ab, hält das Gewissen rein.
Unbeschwert geht man, gebräunt, durchs Leben. Den Besucher
    Lädt das Lächeln weißer Zähne nicht zum Essen ein,

Nein, zum Vergessen. Und den Strand am Ufer der Phäaken
    Säumen Palmen, grüne Säulenreihn. In hellen Villen
Wohnen Leinwand-Engel, diese Ewigschönen, Immerjungen.
    Jeder Friedhof duftet, im WC die Seife, nach Vanille.

*

Freunde, es ist Winter hier, sprich zwanzig Grad im Schatten.
    Fönwind aus den Bergen zaust die Trockenhaube,
Die der Stadt schief aufgestülpt ist als ein gelber Dunst.
    Manchmal sieht man bis in fernste Fernen, was den Glauben

An ein Jenseits abkürzt. Ist das Himmelreich erst irdisch,
    Kann sich jeder schnell in Luft auflösen. Flüchtig
Streift man durch die eine Jahreszeit in vier Quartalen.
    Schon ein Blick zum Horizont macht regenbogensüchtig.

Spätestens im Januar merkt auch der Letzte, farbenblind,
    Daß die Bäume immergrün sind hier in Eden. Dreh dich um:
Zeig dich von der besten Seite zwischen all den heißen Rosten.
    Du entgehst ihm nicht, dem Leben im Solarium.

*

Here a light breeze soughs through your memory every day.
 Bears away singularities, keeps your conscience clear.
You stroll through life, bronzed, at ease. The dazzle
 Of white teeth doesn't invite the visitor to eat,

Rather to forget. And the beach where these Phaeacians consort
 Is lined by palms, green pillars' colonnades.
In pastel villas live screen divas, ever young, of unimpaired allure.
 Every cemetery breathes, like the soap in the comfort station, vanilla.

*

My friends, it is winter here, a pleasant 70 in the shade.
 A wind blows off the coastal hills, ruffling
The hair dryer that sits atop the city like a yellow smog.
 Sometimes you can see miles into the distance, which

Diminishes the belief in an otherworld. If the hereafter is here,
 Then everyone can melt away into thin air.
You encounter the one season spread over four quarters.
 Scanning the horizon, you are surprised to see no rainbow.

By January, at the latest, the least observant of observers
 Will have noticed that the trees are evergreen here in Eden. Turn over:
Show your best side, among all these hot grilles.
 You won't escape it, life in a solarium.

*

Nicht beurlaubt bin ich, nicht verbannt ans andre Ufer.
Was mich herzog, war ein Mythos (einer von den neuen).
Weil hier vieles möglich ist und kaum was wirklich,
Muß man weniger als in der Alten Welt bereuen.

Freunde macht man hier in fünf Minuten, und kaum länger
Dauert auch die Gründung einer Bank — sowie ihr Sturz.
Wenn die Erde bebt und ganze Straßenzüge wackeln,
Scheint das Leben, wie vom Ende her gesehn, sehr kurz.

Schlafen kannst du, wenn es erst vorbei ist. Bis dahin
Hält dich Ungewißheit wach, der Motor unterm Herzen.
Jährlich Wirbelsturm und Waldbrand hinterm Haus, — da ist
Beim Friseur die Schießerei noch einer von den Scherzen.

*

Selbst der Sternenhimmel ist hier anders. Zu den neuen Bildern,
Funkelnd zwischen Leier, Schwan und Schütze,
Zählt ein Cabrio in voller Fahrt, verfolgt von einem Saurier.
Über dem *Revolver* kreist, verkehrtherum, die *Mütze*.

Auf den Hügeln strecken Weltraumteleskope ihre Segelohren
Ufo und Komet entgegen. Eher hier als anderswo
Bäckt man für Besucher aus dem All Begrüßungskuchen.
Kinos sind hier Planetarien, und in manchem Bungalow

Steckt ein Flugleitzentrum für die ersten Raumpatrouillen.
Suchscheinwerfer kreuzen ihre Strahlen nachts zu Chiffren.
Schon vom Flugzeug aus scheint diese Stadt ein Text zu sein,
Den nur Leute mit Facettenaugen einst entziffern.

I'm neither on vacation, nor banished to the other shore.
     What brought me here was a myth (one of the new myths).
Because so much is possible, and hardly anything is real,
     There's less cause for remorse than in the Old World.

You make friends in five minutes, the same time it takes
     To found a bank—and watch it crash.
When the earth shakes, and entire streets wobble,
     Life can seem, as if viewed from beyond the grave, rather brief.

There's time for sleeping afterward. Until then,
     Uncertainty, the engine under the heart, will keep you awake.
Annual cyclones and forest fires beyond the fence—by comparison
     The recent shooting at the barber's is just some light relief.

*

Even the (star-spangled) night sky is different here. Among the new
     Constellations, glittering alongside the Lyre, the Swan, and Sagittarius,
Is a sports car at full tilt, hounded by a Dinosaur.
     Over the Revolver hangs the back-to-front Baseball Cap.

On the hills radio telescopes stretch out their flapping ears
     For UFO and comet. People here will be quicker than elsewhere
To put out the welcome mat for little green visitors.
     Cinemas here double as planetaria, and the odd bungalow

Houses an air traffic control center for the first space patrols.
     At night, swiveling searchlights phase their beams in code.
Seen from the air, the city looks like a scrambled text anyway
     That only beings with polyhedron eyes could ever crack.

Nicht zum Baden laden diese Strände, wüste Landebahnen.
  Beim Spazieren schrickt man auf, wenn da ein Telephon
An der Uferpromenade läutet. Weit und breit kein Mensch . . .
  Durch die Palmenreihen streicht vom Mars ein Celloton.

*

Sechs Sekunden dauert sie genau, die Jetztzeit,
  Zwischen dem, was kommt und dem, was fortan war,
Sagen Ärzte, und es gilt der Hirntest. — Nicht so hier.
  Eher gehn durchs Nadelöhr Kamel *und* Dromedar,

Als daß einer hier zurückblickt, trauernd um sein Gestern.
  ›Chronos?‹ rätseln sie. ›Was ist das? Ein Hormon?‹
›Eine dieser Pillen? Ein verbotner Pornofilm? Ein Cocktail?‹
  In Arkadien weiß man nichts von Noch und Schon.

Und es grenzt an Perversion, wenn jemand sich erinnert
  An den ersten Kuß, erfahrungslos, die Nacht, und dann . . .
Immer ist es Gegenwart, in der die Glückserfinder blinzeln,
  Gut versichert, weil nie enden kann, was nie begann.

*

Kinofilme sind hier, was woanders Erdöl ist und Silikon.
  Aus dem reinen Rohstoff, Zelluloid, wird in den Studios,
Dank des Restlichts aus dem Paradies, was einst ein Atheist,
  Vater der Kommune, *Opium des Volkes* nannte, Religion.

Ja, die Filme sind *der* Clou. Aus scheuen Leutchen zaubern sie
  Im dunklen Saal Unsterbliche, die als Bekannte
Jeden Traum bevölkern. Enkel, hochbegabt, zerstreute Onkel,
  Töchter, schlank wie Modepuppen, scharfe Tanten.

The desert landing strips of the beaches are not for swimming off.
　　And taking a walk, you jump when a telephone shrills
On the promenade. No one around for miles . . .
　　A *thrup* from Mars pulses through the palms.

*

The doctors have conducted tests, and, apparently,
　　What we call the present, the little interstice
Between what was and will be, measures six seconds.—But not here.
　　Camels and dromedaries would sooner pass through the eye of a needle

Than someone look back with sorrow upon his yesterday.
　　"Chronos?" they mutter. "What's that? A hormone supplement?"
"One of those pills? A banned snuff movie? A cocktail?"
　　There's nothing about once and future in Arcadia.

And it seems like some peculiar perversion if someone recollects
　　A first kiss, innocence, the night, and then . . .
It's always in the present that the finders of happiness blink,
　　Comprehensively insured, because nothing can end that never began.

*

Here, not oil and silicon but movies are the local monoculture.
　　The pure raw material, celluloid, is converted in the studios,
Using the remaining light of paradise, into a noted atheist's
　　Definition of religion: *the opium of the people.*

Yes, the film's the thing. Out of shy introverts
　　The auditorium makes immortals who star in every dream.
Gifted grandsons, distracted uncles,
　　Daughters slim as models, blowsy aunts.

Halbgenie und Schönheitskönigin, von hier bis Ephesos
	Kennt man ihre Seitensprünge, Hobbies und die Namen
Von Haustier, Stammlokal und Therapeut, den vollen Speiseplan.
	Auch wer nichts von Delphi weiß, schätzt diese Ehedramen.

Im Geschäft Erfolg zu haben, macht bald frech wie Oscar.
	Ein Skandal poliert den Ruf. Die höchsten Gagen
Bringt der Druck aufs Zwerchfell und die Tränendrüsen.
	Alles ist hier Augentäuschung und Gemütsmassage.

*

Gott, sie machen einen schwach hier, die Korrekten!
	So moralisch kerngesund, daß man vergißt zu schlucken.
Sprüche haben die parat — entwaffnend. Am Buffett,
	Erklärt ein Vegetarier neben dir, aufs Tischtuch spuckend,

Sein Nein zum Fleisch, daß einem Bluthund Tränen kommen.
	Freundlich angefragt, ob man ihm außer Butter
Andre Leckerbissen bieten dürfe, sagt er streng, den Putenbraten
	Verachtend: ›Alles, aber nichts aus einer Mutter . . .‹.

*

Nachts ein Studio. Panoramafenster. Auf der Stelle tretend,
	Sieht man, in den Ohren Stöpsel, Frauen an Metallgeräten,
Die wie Folterwerkzeug aussehn, Streckbank und Garrotte.
	Fitness ist das Zauberwort. Zum eignen Körper beten,

Gilt als Prüfung, die man absolviert nach Plan, voll Inbrunst.
	Jeder ist sein eigner Inquisitor. Herz und Lungen
Werden streng bewacht, daß sie dem Muskelaufbau dienen.
	Was das Hirn macht? Dämmern, sagen böse Zungen.

The half genius and the beauty queen, from here to Ephesus
    Everyone knows their liaisons, hobbies, and the names
Of their pets, their local, and their therapist, the whole shebang.
    Even those who never heard of Delphi follow these dramas.

Success in the business makes you as witty as (Oscar) Wilde.
    A juicy scandal will buff up your reputation.
Pressure on diaphragm and lachrymal glands commands top dollar.
    Everything here is soft soap and trompe l'oeil.

*

By God, the self-righteousness here is stifling!
    So thoroughly moral, it takes your breath away.
The things they come up with. At the buffet,
    The vegetarian behind you spits on the tablecloth,

And sets out his rejection of meat, in terms to make a bloodhound weep.
    Asked nicely back if he would have anything, after another pass
At the turkey, he says, "Yeah, gimme everything,
    But nothing that had a mother."

*

A studio at night. A picture window. Running on the spot,
    Earplugs in, you see women strapped to metal equipment
That resembles torture bench and garrote.
    Fitness is the magic word here. The prayer to one's own body

Is accounted a test that's absolutely de rigueur.
    Everyone his own examiner. Heart and lungs
Are trained to give maximum help to muscle bulk.
    And the brain? Shrivels, say malicious people.

Ist es, weil hier eine ganze Himmelsrichtung abbricht,
　　Daß sie stoisch in Bewegung bleiben auf dem letzten Pier?
Vor sich, was zu keinem Aufbruch mehr verlockt, das Meer.
　　Sind sie besser durchtrainiert in Langeweile hier?

*

Froh zu sei, bedarf es hier des Zahnarzts. ›Welch ein Lächeln . . . . ‹.
　　Denn sein Glück zu machen ist die erste Bürgerpflicht.
Wer es hat, ist kaum zu bremsen. Den Verlierer hält
　　Nichts so sehr bei Laune wie der Glanz der Oberschicht.

Selbstmord gilt als strafbar, ein Delikt. Wer von den Nachbarn
　　Angezeigt wird beim Versuch, sich fortzustehlen,
Hat kaum Zeit, bevor ein Ordnungshüter mit gezieltem Schuß
　　Ihm zuvorkommt. Alles darf man, nur den Tod nicht, wählen.

Gegens Altern läßt man sich versichern, und den Sterbefall
　　Nimmt man gern als Episode und hält tiefgefroren
Einkehr bis zur Auferstehung. Sektenchef und Medienzar
　　Schlafen ihren Lebensrausch aus in den Eistresoren.

Schade nur, daß, wie man hört, die Erde vom Bestatten
　　All der armen Teufel ganz vergiftet ist. Statt Knochendung
Bleibt bei soviel Konservierungsstoffen von den Leichen
　　Nur das Täglichmahl aus Supermärkten in Erinnerung.

*

Wie's mir geht hier in Arkadien, willst du wissen? Prima.
　　Ich vermisse nichts als meinen Schatten. Hinter Hecken
Spielt er manchmal, zwischen Palmen, ein Versteckspiel.
　　Bleib ich stehn, verblüfft, tritt eine Parkuhr aus der Deckung.

Is it because this is as far West as it gets,
    That they remain stoically in motion on the end of the pier?
Ahead of them, tempting no one, the sea.
    Are they better adjusted to boredom here?

*

To be truly happy here, you need a dentist. "Such a dazzling smile . . ."
    Because happiness is the first duty of every citizen.
Whoever is happy, is unstoppable. Nothing so cheers the loser
    As the successful sparklers.

Suicide is accounted a crime. Anyone to whom an interest
    In self-murder is imputed (say, by kindly neighbors)
Has only moments before a lawman shoots him dead.
    You can vote for anything, it seems, but not for death.

You have yourself insured against aging, and death is not seen
    As irrevocable, but more an episode to be waited out
In deep freeze till your comeback. Cult leader and media mogul
    Sleep off their deaths in the safe-deposit box.

Just a pity that the earth is tainted
    By the burial of all the poor devils. What's left of their bodies
Isn't bonemeal, but the everlasting e-numbers
    From the frozen TV dinners in the supermarkets.

*

You want to know how I'm faring in Arcadia. Just fine.
    The only thing I miss is my shadow. It sometimes sticks
Behind a hedge, or between palms, playing hide-and-seek.
    If I stop in bewilderment, a parking meter follows me.

Wehmut überfällt mich nur, wenn ich an Schwarzbrot denke,
  Seine Herbheit und die Kruste wie gefrorne Erde hart.
Daß ein Tag dem andern gleicht, besorgt das Fernsehn,
  Dieses Fenster in den Angsttraum Gegenwart.

Seltsam, daß ich nun hierher gehöre. Manches Photo
  Zeigt mich schamrot, wie erwischt beim Lotosfressen.
Ist das Sonnenbrand? Mit einem Strohhalm in Passionsfrucht-Pfützen
  Schreib ich: ›Grüße aus der Hauptstadt des Vergessens‹.

The only thing that makes me melancholy is the recollection
    Of black bread. Its bitter crust used to taste of earth.
Television, the window into the fearful dream of the present,
    Makes the days more or less indistinguishable.

Odd to think that this is now where I am.
    Photographs show me beet red, as though caught eating lotus.
Is that sunburn? I dip my straw in the passion-fruit slush,
    And write: "Greetings from Oblivion City."

Für Aris Fioretos

So sind die Körper gegangen. In der verlassenen Wohnung
Ist alles posthume Ordnung, von den Spiegeln bereinigt
Bis zu den Flecken im Bad. Unten am Wannengrund
Klebt ein einzelnes Haar, das Relikt einer Tierart,
Die nach der Paarung sich wäscht und die Spuren verwischt.
Wie friedlich die Fensterbretter mit ihren toten Fliegen —
Und doch kommt der Schrecken auch hier
Gern zu Besuch.

In die Ritzen legt er sich, auf Schwellen und Heizungsrippen,
Ein Nest für Insekteneier, ein geruchloser Weihrauch,
Der die Zimmer durchzieht, die Herdplatten schwärzt,
Lauwarm am Boden, in den Vorhangfalten schon kalt.
Hautschuppen sind es, Stäubchen aus einem Reptilienkäfig,
An denen sich zeigt, wer hier schläft. Vom Kalender
Annonciert überm Spülstein, hat die Zeit überdauert
Irgendein Montag.

Unter den Dielen liegt Bauschutt, und an den Möbeln ist nichts
Menschlich, außer der Zähigkeit, die sie geschaffen hat,
Den geripphaften Tisch, das Ensemble verknöcherter Stühle,
Die solang keine Hüfte mehr warmhielt und keine Hand.
Im Waschbecken trocknet, im Wasserhahn krümmt sich
Die Illusion vom erleichterten Leben. Komfort
Ruft aus den Ecken ein Hausgeist, der sich versteckt hält,
Wo sonst der Staubsauger aufheult
Im animalischen Dreck.

for Aris Fioretos

The bodies are gone. A posthumous tidiness reigns
In the empty apartment, spring-cleaned from the mirrors
To the stains in the bath. At the bottom of the tub
Curls one single hair, last surviving trace of a species
That cleans up after itself and washes after mating.
How peaceful are the windowsills with their dead flies—
But even here terror likes to call.

It insinuates itself into crevices, thresholds, and radiator ribs,
A hatchery for insect eggs, an odorless incense
Wafting through the room, blackening the stove rings,
Lukewarm at floor level, cooling in the curtain pleats.
Scales of skin it is, sweepings from a reptile cage
That show who sleeps here. To go by the kitchen calendar
Hanging over the sink, some Monday or other
Has come and gone.

There is builders' rubble under the floorboards, and nothing human
About the furniture, save the tenacity with which it was assembled,
The skeletal table, the clutch of ossified chairs,
So long unwarmed by either hand or behind.
The illusion of mod cons is dried up in the sink,
Wrung out in the windings of taps. Comfort
Summons a shy house ghost out of the corners,
Where at other times the vacuum reveled
In the bestial squalor.

Dorthin zurück kehrt, manchmal nach Tagen, nach Wochen,
Erstaunt, der hier wohnt. Mit dem Schlüsselbund fällt
Sein Blick auf neutralen Boden, bevor er sich fängt
Im geschlossenen Mauerwerk. Gebannt steht er da,
Für Augenblicke sich fremd wie vor den spurlosen Fugen
Der Kaltwasserbecken Pompejis, vor der zerkratzten Wand
Im *Haus der Verkohlten Möbel*, den Obszönitäten,
Dunkel und fleischlos.

So sind die Schatten verschwunden. Und vom Stein aufgesaugt
Ist der schmale Schweißrand, den in der Julihitze am Mittag
Der Fuß einer Römerin hinterließ. Die Kammern alle,
Durch Türen verbunden, nachdem sie geräumt sind,
Kennt keiner sie wieder. Vor versammelter Leere
Ist jedes Rosa getilgt, und der Rost an den Rohren bleibt
Länger frisch als in der Küche das Fischblut, auf neuen Tellern
Der Augapfelglanz.

Doch in den Abfalleimern keimt Leben. Und manchmal bricht
Beim Durchwühlen der Tüten ein Fingernagel. Ein Mißgriff
Zieht einen Splitter ins Fleisch. Eine Schublade klemmt,
Weil ein Photo, das dich als Säugling zeigt, festhängt
Mit der Beharrlichkeit eines Gegenstandes im Traum.
Pflanzen, im Schrank vertrocknet, dementieren den Frieden
Einer tickenden Wanduhr. Von überall höhnt es:
›Sieh, was draus wird . . . .‹.

Das steife Handtuch, zum Beispiel, am Haken, und an der Tür
Ein Paar Halbschuh, bis hierher getragen. Oder die Bürste,
Grau mit dem Abdruck vom Zähneputzen — ein Nachlaß
Zur Lebzeit, erspäht durch ein Schlüsselloch,
Ein Archiv kleiner Tode, das jederzeit auflösbar ist.
Bis etwas anfällt, das keiner vermißt hat, — ein Röntgenbild
Zwischen gelben Rezepten in einer Krankenakte,

After an interval of days, in some cases weeks, the inhabitant
Returns here, to his own surprise. His glance falls—along with
His key ring—to the indifferent floor, before catching itself
On the resolute walls. He stands there fascinated,
As much a stranger to himself as he would be
Before the grouted frigidarium of Pompeii, or the scribbled walls
Of the House of Charred Furniture, the dark
And juiceless obscenities.

The shades have fled. Printed on the stone
Is the narrow edge of sweat that a Roman woman's foot
Left one July noon. No one could identify
The interconnecting chambers, once they're vacated.
All trace of pink has gone from the assembled emptiness,
Though the rust of the pipes keeps its freshness longer
Than the fishes' blood in the kitchen,
The ocular gleam of clean plates.

Life burgeons in dustbins. Only sometimes a fingernail breaks
While rummaging through the plastic bags. A false movement
Drills a splinter into the flesh. A desk drawer jams
Because, with the insistence of an object in a dream,
An infant photograph of yourself keeps sticking.
Plants, desiccated in a cupboard, deny the peaceably
Ticking grandfather clock. From everywhere comes the derisive:
"You see what comes of . . ."

For instance, the towel dangling stiffly on its hook,
Or the pair of shoes, parked by the door,
That got you this far. Or again, the toothbrush,
Gray with use, a living relic, spied through a keyhole,
An archive of tiny deaths that might be broken up at any time.
Till something turns up that no one missed—an X-ray
In among the yellow bills in a medical file,

Ein Negativ, das den eigenen Schädel zeigt,
Im Knochen den Bruch.

Das Souvenir eines Unfalls, — und durch Bestrahlung ist
Alles Fleisch restlos beseitigt worden. Weiß auf dem Film
Liegt ein Schleier, um leere Augenhöhlen der Zigarettenrauch
Eines paffenden Engels. Ein Dreieck klafft
Anstelle der Nase. Durch den verdunkelten Mund
Schiebt sich das All. Und dieses Grinsen, in Kalzium gefaßt,
Ist das erste Gesicht und das letzte, aus dem
Nichts mehr zurückblickt.

Denn mit den Wimpern gestrichen, mit den geduldigen Lidern,
Sind auch die Augen, Haut und Haar aufgebraucht
Wie aus den Drüsen der Stoff für Romane, die Tränen,
Und jede Falte. Auf die man so gerne gebissen hatte,
Die Lippen sind fort. Und verschluckt ist die Zunge
Hinterm Gebiß. Doch in den Jahren nachher
(Oder waren es Stunden) blieb, wo der Hammer ihn traf,
Der verbogene Nagel im Putz. Durch den Anstrich sichtbar,
War an der Decke der Wasserfleck. Blau wie am ersten Tag
Stand die Vase im Fenster, das Veilchengrab, lag in der Schale
Ein rundes Stück Seife, unbenutzt. Und die Spur von Gebrauch
An Messern und Flaschenhälsen war eine falsche Fährte
In der verlassenen Wohnung. Vor kahlen Wänden,
Flackernd im Röntgenlicht, zeugte nichts mehr
Von den Balancen der Körper, verschwunden
Im Kommen und Gehn.

A negative showing your own skull,
With the break in the bone.

The souvenir of an accident—radiation
Has stripped away all the flesh. A white veil
Lies on the film, an angel's cigarette smoke swirls
Round the empty eye sockets. A triangle gapes
In lieu of a nose. Space is inhaled
Through the dark oral cavity. And that calcium grin
Is both your ur-face and your last, from which
Nothing looks back at you.

Eyes, skin, and hair are all abolished,
Canceled along with the eyelashes and the dutiful eyelids,
As are the tears—lifeblood of fiction—in their ducts and glands,
And every wrinkle. The lips you used to gnaw are gone.
Swallowed up the tongue behind the teeth.
But all through the subsequent years (or weeks),
The bent nail stays in the plaster just exactly
Where the hammer drove it. The damp patch on the ceiling
Shines dully through the paint. Blue as on the first day,
The vase, final resting place of generations of violets, stands in the window,
A small coin of soap lies pristine in its dish. All signs of use
On knives and bottlenecks are a false trail
In the abandoned apartment. Against bare walls,
Flickering in the X-ray illumination, nothing remains
To recall the poise of bodies, vanished
In the come and go.

Kurz und bös, ich bin großgeworden im öden Schlamassel,
Der allem droht, was sich verkennt. Unter Spatzen und Spitzeln
War ich auf leerem Appellplatz tollkühn, schweigsam in stummer
    Masse.
Ein Clown, siebenzüngig, ein Chorknabe, scharf auf die zynischen Witze.
Ungefragt sprechend wie andere spucken, beiseite
Hab ich die Schocks der Ohnmacht verleugnet mit schwarzem Humor.
Denn die Historie war mir von Nachteil, des Menschen Pleite.
Dort wo ich aufwuchs, kam Größe nur in Legenden vor.

Gleich mit dem Lesen hab ich Verstellung gelernt, in frühen Etüden
Unter Frömmlern den Thomas, vor Ketzern Sankt Petrus gespielt.
Ich sah die Null hochdekoriert, unter Zwergen den Riesen ermüden.
Der geborene Deserteur: lieber tot als auf Herzen gezielt.
Ich hab aus Panzern gekotzt, in Kasernen mich in den Schlaf geheult,
Im Zeltlager überm Kübel mein schiefes Grinsen rasiert.
Mehr als mein Knie vom Fußball war bald die Seele zerbeult.
Oft kam ich heim mit dem Meineid ›Schon gut. Nichts passiert.‹
Ich habe Akten gestempelt vorm Reißwolf, Bäume grün angepinselt,
Phantasiert über alles, und manches, was es im Traum nicht mal gibt.
Utopia zum Beispiel . . . Seit Morus spielt das auf rauhen Inseln.
In den Neubausteppen hab ich den ersten mageren Körper geliebt,
Lang vor den Lilien den Müllwind geschnüffelt, die Dünste
Aus Kantine und Schlachthof und den Gestank voller Züge.
Ein Palast in Betongrau, das war die *Schule der Schönen Künste.*
Und aus den Klassen sang es: Ihr Musen, vergebt, wenn ich lüge . . .
Alle Bedenkzeit der Welt hab ich gehabt, doch es gab nichts,
Was das Kopfschütteln lohnte. Die neuen Bibeln warn das Papier
Nicht mehr wert, und fürs Leben die einzige Lehre: die des Verzichts.

In a rotten nutshell, I grew up amid the barrenness and confusion
That lie in wait for anything that mistakes itself. Among stoolies and
    spies,
I risked my neck on the empty parade ground, kept *shtum* in the silent
    masses,
A clown with seven tongues, a choirboy with an ear for cynical jokes.
Unasked, I spoke as others might spit, out of the side of my mouth,
And masked my own shocking helplessness with black humor.
History was no use to me, all it showed was human failings anyway.
Where I grew up, greatness was something you read about in saints' lives.

Imbibed with my reading was hypocrisy. In a few infantile études,
I played doubting Thomas to the devout, Peter the Rock to heretics.
I saw the zero beribboned, and the colossus ground down by dwarves.
The born deserter: sooner die than take aim at the heart.
I puked out of tanks, cried myself to sleep in barracks.
Shaved my skewed grin over a bucket, under canvas.
I did in my knee at soccer, but my soul fared much worse.
How often I would come home with the lie on my lips: "All right.
    Nothing much."
I stacked files to feed the shredder, applied green paint to trees,
Fantasized about everything under the sun, and a few things that aren't.
Utopia, for instance . . . Ever since Thomas More, those isles have been
    bleak.
In the concrete wastes, I embraced my first scrawny body.
For want of lilies, I sniffed the garbage on the breeze, guzzled the aromas
Of canteen and abattoir, and the stench of overcrowded trains.
A palace in gray concrete was my École des Beaux-Arts,
Where the classrooms chorused: Muse, excuse me if I lie . . .
I had all the time in the world for reflection, but there was nothing
To shake a stick at. The new Bibles weren't worth the paper
They were printed on, and the only lesson for living was: Do without.

Eine Knastlitanei. Lang ists her, und sieh da, ich bin immer noch hier.
Wo Staaten wie Sandburgen rutschten, die Illusion hoch im Kurs stand,
War es Instinkt, die Musik lauter zu stellen und leise,
Die zwei, drei Zeilen zu summen, die dieses Land
Unter Wasser setzten. So ging ich allein auf die Reise,
Zurück durch die Brennesselfelder, die Dörfer, entgegen den Trecks,
Im Ohr noch den russischen Laut des Sergeanten: ›Dawai, dawai!‹.
Nostalgie, eine fistelnde Stimme, empfahl mir *Bevor du verreckst,*
Irgendwas Fernes. Die Brandung am Strand von Hawaii?

A prison *règlement*. It was all a long time ago, and lo, I'm still here.
Where states melted away like sand castles, and illusion was at a
    premium,
It was second nature to me to turn the music up, and softly hum
The two or three lines that were sufficient to put the country
Under water. As I embarked on my sentimental journey
Through nettle fields and villages, the other way to the general exodus,
The sergeant's Russian bawl: *"Dawai, dawai!"* was still ringing in my ear.
Nostalgia's falsetto recommended something exotic before you hand in
Your dinner pail. What say the Hawaiian beaches?

Einmal im Halbschlaf . . . zwischen Nehmen und Geben
Habe ich meine Hände gesehn, ihre gelbrote Haut
Wie die eines Andern, einer Leiche im Schauhaus.
Beim Essen hielten sie Messer und Gabel, das Werkzeug
Des Kannibalen, mit dem die Jagd sich vergessen ließ
Und das Getöse beim Schlachten.

                     Leer wie der Teller
Lag eine Handfläche vor mir, der fleischige Ballen
Des letzten Affen, dem alles erreichbar geworden war
In einer Welt von Primaten. Mantegna vielleicht
Hätte sie unverklärt malen können in ihrer Grausamkeit,
Diese fettigen Schwielen.

                  Was war die Zukunft,
Die aus den Handlinien folgte, Glück oder Unglück,
Gegen den Terror der Poren, in denen der Schweiß stand
Wie die Legende vom stillen Begreifen auf einer Stirn.

Half asleep once . . . between giving and taking,
I saw my hands, their mottled red and yellow
Like those of a stranger, a stiff in a morgue.
At mealtimes, they plied knife and fork, the tools
Of the cannibal, who used them to forget the chase
And the screams of the slaughtered.
                                        In front of me
Lay a palm as empty as my plate, the fleshy mound
Of the last of the apes, who found everything within reach
In a world of primates. Mantegna, perhaps,
Might have been able to paint them untransfigured in their horror,
Those fatty calluses.
                        What was the future
Predicted in the lines of that hand, love or fortune,
Compared to the terror of the pores, steeped in sweat
Like the myth of silent understanding on a forehead.

I

Raumlos, Erinnerung . . . und keine Stadt,
An die man sich, heimkehrend, halten kann.
Wo dieser Vorwärtstraum ein Ende hat,
In welchem *Wann?*

Den ersten Fluß verteilt das Wassernetz
In jede Unterkunft. Auf kaltem Heizungsrohr
Stehn rostrot Tropfen bis zuletzt.
Spüllärm im Ohr

Reißt das Verzeichnis früher Straßen fort.
Die man im Schlaf fand, Plätze, garantiert
Vom Laufenlernen . . . sind jetzt allerorts
Evakuiert.

I

Memory has no real estate . . . no city
where you come home and you know where you are.
Is there no when
where this rampaging dream will rest?

Your first river is distributed
round the houses by the water board. On the chilly heating pipes
there are the rust-red drips even now.
A roaring in your ears

washes away the A–Z of early streets.
Those places you used to find in your sleep, where you took
your first faltering steps . . . see them all
evacuated.

II

Dresden ist lange her,
Ein Festsaal gestern, vor der neuen Blöße
Unglaublich, ein Gerücht von Größe,
Ein Nachruf im Bericht des deutschen Heers.

Taghell für eine Nacht,
Ist das dieselbe Stadt im Tal, dieselbe
(Im Anflug ein Las Vegas an der Elbe)
Wie der Pilot sie sah in Phosphorpracht?

Längst war sie todgeweiht,
Bewohnt noch, schon vergessen von den letzten
Flüchtigen Mietern, die Erynnien hetzten
Aus der urbanen in die Aschenzeit.

II

Dresden is long ago,
yesterday's ballroom, a little implausible
in the new plainness, a large-scale rumor,
an obituary in the official chronicles of the German army.

So and so many candlepower for one night,
is it the same city in the valley, the same
(approaching some Las Vegas on the Elbe)
as the pilot saw in its phosphorescent glory?

It was at one and the same time
long doomed, still inhabited, and already forgotten
by the last of its fly-by-night tenants, the Furies flitting
from civilization to ashes.

III

Denn das Wort kommt zu spät, das sie ruft,
Die am Stadtrand begrabene Stadt.
Wo ein Müllberg sich breit macht, der lokale Vesuv
Schwarzen Rauch ausstößt überm Kiefernwald, hat
Längst die Erde ihn wieder, den Namen, und nichts
Unterscheidet das Nest noch von anderen Nestern,
Die auf Asche gebaut sind, auf soliden Verzicht.

Unter Schuttbergen sinkt, unter Null, alles Gestern
Aus Terrassen und Kuppeln, barocker Bau.
Wie ein Uhrglas von innen beschlägt und wird matt,
Liegt verregnet im Tal unter grauem Tau
Zwischen Himmel und Grundriß der Rest von Stadt.
Und lebt weiter im Flüstern, in Gerüchten aus Stein,
Die vom Fürstenzug handeln. Italienische Luft
Heißt hier *Smog um Pompeji* oder *Nördlichster Wein*.
Doch das Wort kommt zu spät, das sie ruft.

III

Because the word celebrating it
has come too late, the city buried at the city's edge.
Where a rubbish dump looms, the local Vesuvius
spews black smoke over the pine woods, the earth
has reclaimed it, and there's nothing
to distinguish this place from other places
built on ashes, on solid renunciation.

The terraced, domed, and baroque post
subsides, subzero, under piles of trash.
Like the condensation furring a watch glass from within,
whatever's left of the city lies between sky and outline
in a rainy valley under gray dew.
And there it lives on in whispers, in rumors of stone,
about the ducal procession. Italian air
here goes by the name of Pompeiian smog or northernmost vines.
But the word celebrating it comes too late.

IV

Täglich vom Starren auf den Fluß (nach Jahren)
Tränten die Augen uns. Willkommen, Elbe.
In dieser trägen, gelblich braunen Brühe
Ist meine Mutter noch als Kind geschwommen.
Da lag kein Ölglanz auf dem Haar. Dasselbe
Gemeine Licht brach durch die Nachkriegsfrühe.
Das Stadtbild hatte etwas abgenommen,
Am Ufer hockten Angler noch in Scharen,
Und durch das Elbtal ging kaum Schiffsverkehr.
Ein Fluß, was ist das, wenn die Stadt versinkt
Vor seinen Wellen, die den Großbrand spiegeln.
Ein trüber Himmel, der mit toten Fischen blinkt,
Ein Notausgang, die Tür mit sieben Siegeln, —
Reklame für das nächste offne Meer?

IV

Our eyes teared up every day (and years later)
from gazing at the river. Hello, Elbe.
My mother used to swim there as a girl,
in that sluggish yellow-brown soup.
There was no shimmer of oil on her hair. The same
low light broke through the postwar days.
The vista of the city was somewhat diminished,
but fishermen still hunkered by the score on the banks,
and there wasn't much in the way of shipping.
A river, but what's a river when the city sinks
before its waves, reflecting back the blaze.
A murky sky, all ablink with dead fishes,
an emergency exit, the door with seven seals—
a plug for the nearest open sea?

V

Und nachts die stille deutsche Stadt,
In die man einfuhr mit dem Zug vom Norden,
Setzte mit jeder Straßenlampe neue Fragezeichen

Und hinter jeden Satz den Punkt, — mit wieviel Watt?
›Was ist aus Xanadu nach Kublai Khan geworden?‹
›Wer sind die Leute, die dort mausgrau schleichen?‹

Islamabad im Elbtal . . . Eine Phantasie-Moschee
Erhob sich dort und rief die Hörigen zum Fasten,
Vom Schlachthoftürmchen bis zum Großen Garten.

Doch schon am Bahnhof hörte man das erste ›Nee.‹
Und sah Giraffenhälse, lange Flutlichtmasten,
Die leicht geneigt sich um ein Fußballstadion scharten.

Das Blaue Wunder hieß flußaufwärts eine Brücke,
Die einem nichts erklärte. Immerhin, sie stand
Gußeisern, nützlich in der Nachkriegsdschungelstadt.

An den entblößten Ufern, braun in Einzelstücken,
Stieß man auf wuchtigen Barock. Wer wollte, fand
Im kalten Mondlicht hier sein Angkor Vat.

V

And at night the silent German city,
austerely north-facing station,
using street lamps sparingly as question marks

and behind every sentence a period—how many watts?
"What became of Xanadu post–Kubla Khan?"
"Who are those gray people, scrabbling around like mice?"

Like Islamabad-on-the-Elbe . . . The fantasy mosque
puffed out its cheeks and summoned—from the abattoir turrets
to the big garden—the faithful to the fast.

You hadn't left the station before you heard the first *"Nee."*
And saw giraffe necks, long floodlight stanchions,
craning peculiarly, hunching round the soccer stadium.

The Blue Wonder was the name of a bridge upstream,
a somewhat unmotivated construction. Still, it stood there,
handy and cast iron, useful in the postwar jungle of the city.

Along the scuffed banks, worn brown in parts,
you still encountered massy baroque. Some souls might find
their personal Angkor Wat there in the chilly moonlight.

VI

Meiner Großmutter Dora W.

Und als der erste Angriff kam, sie lag
Im Krankenhaus mit Scharlach. Der Alarm
Riß viele aus dem Schlaf. Vom Glutwind warm
War draußen Winter, und die Nacht war Tag.

Gespenster, die im weißen Nachthemd spuken,
Rannten sie barfuß an die Elbewiesen.
. . . — Panik, ein Luftstrom aus den Feuerluken,
Bevor aus allen Wolken die Posaunen bliesen.

Und als der zweite Angriff kam, verschwand
Die Stadt im Stummfilm, und kein Schatten fiel
Als sie verbrannte durch die Flammenwand,
Den einen Falle und den andern Ziel.

Aus einer Nacht im Zwanzigsten Jahrhundert
Flogen Maschinen eine zweite Steinzeit an.
In manchem Kellergrab, ein Höhlenwunder,
Fand man verbacken Kind und Frau und Mann.

Und als der dritte Angriff kam, sie ging
Gefaßt im Flüchtlingszug, auf schwachen Beinen
In eine Nachwelt ein. Da war kein Weinen,
Das auf den Trümmern noch verfing.

VI

to my grandmother, Dora W.

When the first wave of bombers came, she was
In hospital with scarlet fever. The air-raid alarm
Tore many from their dreams. The winter air grew warm,
And the night was bright as day.

Like ghosts in their white nightshirts,
They ran barefoot to the Elbe meadows . . .
Panic, a surge of air from the bomb bays,
Before the angels trumpeted from on high.

And when the second wave of bombers came,
The city vanished into a silent film, and no shadow fell
As it burned through the wall of flame,
That was objective to some, and a trap to others.

On one twentieth-century night, planes
Delivered a second stone age.
The odd bomb shelter, like the tomb behind the stone,
Housed were man, wife, and child, all done to a crisp.

And when the third wave came, she was walking
Calmly in the line of refugees, on tottering legs
To the afterlife. There were no tears,
Nothing left to cry with in whatever was left.

VII

Ach, Hiroshima war nur zweite Wahl.
Premiere haben sollte sie (sagt man) in Dresden,
Die Bombe, die heut jedes Schulkind malt —

Der Riesenpilz, die weltberühmte Abschiedsgeste
Der alten Opernhimmel. Wieviel schöner
Wäre der strahlende Bovist hier aufgeblüht

Über der sandsteinhellen Residenz als Krönung
Barocker Baukunst. Aufs Gemüt
Schlägt die Vision, wie stilvoll *hier* die legendäre
Finale Wolke aufgegangen wäre.

VII

Hiroshima, it seems, was Plan B.
The premiere was to have been in Dresden
For the bomb that every schoolkid draws nowadays —

The giant mushroom, the world famous parting gesture
Of the old opera skies. How much more beautifully
The dazzling toadstool would have sprouted here,

Over the pale sandstone residence, as the logical pinnacle
Of so much Baroque. Moving, the vision
Of what might have been, the legendary final cloud
Harmoniously exploding *here*.

VIII

Zerrissen ist das Blatt vorm Mund. Geschichte, —
Geht mir der Staubwind wirklich nah,
Der alles auslöscht? Und daß man verzichte
Im Namen dessen was geschah

Auf den Vermeer (verbrannt), den Bach (verschollen),
War es das wert? Daß ganze Städte,
Aus denen Züge zur Vernichtung rollten,
Brachflächen wurden an den Ufern Lethes.

Gepflügt wird hier mit Bomben, und kein Bauer
Kennt sich mehr aus. Der Löwenzahn
Nimmt den Figuren auf dem Fries die Dauer.
Was geht Zerstörung, oben, einen Maulwurf an?

VIII

Nothing veiled anymore, history,
The hot, dusty wind that eradicates,
And I care. And in the name of what happened there
One gives up the Vermeer (burned)

And the Bach (disappeared).
Was it worth it? That whole cities,
From which the death transports rolled
Became wastelands on Lethe's banks.

The plowing is done with bombs here, and no farmer
Is familiar. Dandelion
Chews up the figures on the frieze.
What does the mole care about the damage he does?

Dresden, die Restestadt . . . ein Hinterhalt
Für Engel, die der Krieg hier internierte
Vorm Rückflug. Unter Sandstein und Basalt
Sind sie begraben worden. Zirkustiere

Waren die letzten, die sie fliehen sahn ins Feuer.
Ein Pferd, das rechnen konnte, und der Tiger,
Den William Blake rief. Keins ein Ungeheuer,
Verglichen mit den smarten Jungs, den Fliegern,

Die sich im Tiefflug Mensch und Bestie holten.
Ihr Kunststück brauchte kein Trapez, kein Netz
Hoch über der Manege. Die verkohlten
Apostel auf den Dächern stehn entsetzt.

IX

Dresden, leftover city . . . a death trap
For angels, left stranded here by the War
Before they could fly back. Buried under sandstone
And basalt. Circus animals

Were the last creatures they saw fleeing
Into the fire. A horse that could count,
And Blake's tyger. None of them a monster,
Compared to the smart boys, the pilots,

Who went after man and beast on diving raids.
They did their stunts without a net or trapeze
Above the arena. The charred
Apostles on the roofs stand there in dismay.

X

›Nach einer Sekunde schon war sie
stundenlang fort.‹

PROUST / UNTERWEGS ZU SWANN

Stadt im Flockenwirbel vor beschlagner Brille —
Bei der ersten Heimkehr ging sie unbemerkt verloren.
Nur in Weihnachtsliedern gab es solche Stille
Wie in dieser Nacht am Bahnhofsplatz. Mit roten Ohren
Stand ein Milchgesicht im Schnee, und das warst du,
Dank des Urlaubsscheins auf freiem Fuß. Die Uniform
Ließ nur kleine Sprünge zu. Doch für ein Känguruh
War bei Minusgraden die Geduld enorm.

Keiner kam, dich abzuholen. In der eignen Stadt
War man endlich fremd. Das Leben hinter den Gardinen,
Die Burleske, bis der letzte sagt, *Jetzt bin ich satt . . . ,*
Sah vom Stehplatz aus wie große Pantomime.
Niemals wieder hätte man soviel gegeben,
Wenn die Schöne in der Straßenbahn, befehlsgewohnt,
Nur gelächelt hätte. Sah man doch, Familienleben
Ging auch weiter ohne den verlornen Sohn.

X

After no more than a second, it was as though
she'd been gone for hours.

—PROUST, *SWANN'S WAY*

City in the blizzard beyond your misted glasses—
your first visit home, you lost them and didn't miss them.
You'd have to go to Christmas carols
to find silence as thick as that outside the station.
A pair of red ears and a pale face in the snow, and that was you.
At liberty, thanks to an army exeat.
The uniform restricted you to small jumps for joy.
But for a kangaroo you showed a lot of patience, out in the deep freeze.

No one was there to meet you. In your own city,
you were a stranger at last. The life behind net curtains,
the burlesque that carried on till the last one said, that's it, I've had
    it . . . ,
from your standing seat, it looked like a big panto.
Never again would you have prayed so fervently
for the beauty in the streetcar, used to orders, to flash
you a smile. Anyway, as you soon saw, family
life went on without the prodigal—what was he now?

XI

Im Ernst, Max, von so einer Stadt
Träumt man leicht, bis man schwarz wird.
Auch ohne Tränen sieht man die Farben zerfließen.

Über dem grausam zerschlissnen Brokat
Benimmt selbst der Himmel sich kindisch.
Doch was soll's, in die neuen wetterfesten Markisen

Sind Geschichten kaum noch gewebt.
Nur die schwarzgelben Wappen schlagen
Überall durch den Stoff, als sei gar nichts geschehn.

Soll man, wenn dort ein Zeppelin schwebt,
Melancholisch werden beim Anblick der Elbe?
Niemand, nach hundert Jahren, ließe sich soweit gehn.

XI

Im Ernst, Max—no kidding now—you can dream
of a city like that till you're blue in the face.
You can watch the colors dissolve, without even crying.

Above the slashed brocade,
even the sky is infantile, and pouts.
But what's the use, they've stopped weaving tapestries

in the new waterproof marquees.
Only the old black and yellow favors continue to
poke through the material, as though nothing had happened.

If there's a zeppelin hanging aloft,
should the sight of the Elbe make you melancholy?
No one, in a hundred years, would go that far.

ERKLÄRTE
NACHT

(2002)

>*Du kannst ja nach Berlin fahren. Da bist du schon einmal gewesen.*<

KIERKEGAARD, DIE WIEDERHOLUNG

Dezembermorgen. Im Taxi, an Friedhofsmauern vorüberfahrend,
Überrascht dich dein Neid. >*Die* haben's geschafft.<
In den Augen, vom Licht aufgestemmt, reibt es wie nasser Sand.
Der Fahrer nestelt am Rosenkranz. Du siehst nur die Bahren
In den Schaufenstern, Trödel, hinter gelben Gardinen, gerafft.
Dann beginnst du zu zählen. Die Finger an jeder Hand
Reichen nicht aus — so viele Bestattungsfirmen gibt es entlang
Der Strecke von der Haustür zum Bahnhof. Schamlos ihr Werben,
Schwarz auf weiß, um die Toten von morgen, in harten Sätzen.
Alles ist rechtwinklig hier. Kreuze und Gitter brechen den Drang,
Als Samurai, ein Schwert in der Magengrube, zu sterben.
Die Bäcker haben den Brotteig verrührt. Die Metzger wetzen
Die Klingen vor Arbeitsbeginn. Obst glänzt in Stiegen, sortiert.
Das Taxameter, in Zwanzigerschritten, springt mit dem Geld um,
Das sich unendlich langsam verdient, mit elegischen Zeilen.
Fröstelnd das Hirn, exklusiv vom Zynismus der Zeit penetriert,
Reagiert mit Schläfrigkeit. Der Fahrgast erwidert stumm
Im Rückspiegel den Blick des Chauffeurs. Er muß sich beeilen,
Wenn er den Zug nicht verpassen will. Im Autoradio raunt
Eine sachliche Stimme die Weltnachrichten um sechs Uhr drei.
Irgendwo steigt jetzt ein Börsencoup, irgendwo platzt ein Scheck.
>Schon mal vorausgedacht?< pöbelt in Fettschrift ein *Sarg Discount*.
Am Straßenrand blitzt ein Leben auf, einzeln und — schon vorbei.
>Lange trauern hat keinen Zweck. Wir schaffen die Leiche weg.<

BERLIN POSTHUMOUS

You can always go to Berlin. Remember, you've been there before.

KIERKEGAARD, REPETITION

December morning. Driving past the cemetery walls in the taxi,
You feel a strange pang of envy. *"Their* worries are over."
In your eyes, forced apart by light, you have a sensation as of wet sand.
The driver is fingering his worry-beads. You see nothing but biers
In the windows, junk, behind yellow drawn curtains.
And then you begin counting. The fingers of both hands
Are not enough for all the undertakers on the stretch
Between your front door and the station, all hustling shamelessly
For the dead of tomorrow. A cutthroat business, evidently.
Everything here is right angles. Crosses and latticework cure you
Of your yen to die as a samurai with a sword in your guts.
The bakers have kneaded their dough. Different fruit gleams in flats.
The butchers are whetting their blades before getting to work.
The taximeter skips ahead twenty cents at a time—money it takes
Forever to earn if what you do for a living is turn hexameters.
A delicate shiver in your brain, the effect of so much cynicism
Taken on an empty stomach, first thing in the morning.
Silently you catch the eye of the driver in the rearview mirror.
He will have to step on it if you're not to miss your train.
6:03, a low voice gabbles financial news on the car radio.
A raiding party on some stock exchange, someone else's credit rating
    dives.
"Ever considered the future?" the bold print mugs you in *Coffins for all*
    the Family.
On the pavement edge, a life flashes by—a blur and gone.
"What's the sense in endless moping. Just leave us to do the coping."

Nicht nur das Zentrum, menschenleer am Sonntagvormittag,
Die Briefe, gestempelt mit dem Vermerk *Empfänger unbekannt*,
Das Meeresrauschen im Telephonhörer, in die Stille das ›Bitte?‹
Die tausenden Autos, von den Besitzern verlassen am Straßenrand,
Auch die Reklametafeln mit den Dichterplagiaten, die keiner liest,
In den Parks, grell beschmiert, die Monumente der Schulbuchidole,
Dies alles und manches, wovor man die Augen gern schließt,
Nährt den Verdacht. So also sieht, aufgeschwollen zur Metropole,
Der Ort aus, an dem man den Gott einst begrub wie einen Hund.
Arkadien, Friedhof der Himmlischen, ihm gleicht jede Stadt,
Wo der Tod ein- und ausgeht, das Leben auf privatisiertem Grund.
Von wegen Idylle, Landschaft der Seligen, bukolisches Reservat.
Was immer Hirten besangen, wovon die Reisenden träumten —
Dies ist der Schauplatz. *City* und *gorod*, *metropolis* oder *ville*.
Hier geht man, sein eigener Geist, unter stoischen Bäumen,
Ein gläserner Mensch, schlaflos, sich spiegelnd im Vielzuviel.
Den Takt geben Blicke, urbane Reflexe, nicht die Eklogen,
In denen Daphnis flirtete, Milon und Lakon einander beschützten.
Man spürt sein Skelett, Vertebrat im Vibrato der Brückenbogen,
Verliert das Gesicht, geblendet vom metallischen Glanz der Pfützen,
Und ist doch nirgends so heimisch. Erst hier, im gewohnten Exil,
Wo man nachs in sein Mauseloch kroch, gab es Krümel von Glück.
Wann sonst, wenn nicht im dichten Verkehr, unterwegs ohne Ziel,
War man je so vital, so dem faulen posthumen Frieden entrückt?

It's not just the city center, deserted on Sunday morning,

The letters, branded with the stamp *not known at this address*,

The sea-surge in the phone, and the irked yell of "Pardon?"

The thousands of cars abandoned at the roadside by their owners;

It's also the advertising hoardings with the poetic borrowings that no
one reads,

The defaced monuments to boyhood heroes in the parks,

All this and much more, from which you prefer to avert your gaze—

Well, it gives you pause. This, then, swollen to metropolitan dimensions,

Is what it looks like, the place where they buried god like a dog.

Arcadia, celestial cemetery, a model for every city

Where death comes and goes, and life stutters on privatized astroturf.

Forget your idylls, your landscape of the blest, your bucolic reservations.

Whatever the shepherds sang, or travelers dreamed—

This here's the place for you. *City* and *gorod, metropolis* or *ville.*

Here you promenade your own soul, beneath stoical trees,

A glass man, insomniac, reflected in so much excess.

The tempo's set by glances, flashing eye-contacts, not eclogues

Of flirtatious Daphne, Milon and Lakon closer than a pair of brothers.

You can feel the buzz in your bones, your spine in the judder of the
arcades,

Lose your face, dazzled from the metallic upgleam of the puddles,

But where else is home? It was only ever here, in this familiar exile

When you crept into your rathole at night, that you tasted a few crumbs
of joy.

When else, if not in the human flock, maundering without purpose,

Did you feel so alive, so cut adrift from the moldering posthumous
peace?

NOTES

"PORTRAIT OF THE ARTIST AS A YOUNG BORDER DOG (NOT COLLIE)"

73 *"Like a dog"*: The last words of Franz Kafka's novel *The Trial*: "Like a dog! he said, it was as though the shame would outlive him."

77 *"Nothing"*: Comment from a border-patrol officer who served on the Berlin Wall for thirty years.

85 *"half* enfant perdu": Character from Heinrich Heine's eponymous poem about a doomed sentry on the front lines.

93 See *"i due occhi della storia"* allegory from *Scienza Nuova*, the principal work of the philosopher Giambattista Vico (1668–1744).

"THE MISANTHROPE ON CAPRI"

195 Refers to the emperor Tiberius (42 BC–37 AD). From his villa on Capri, which today is inhabited by lizards, he ruled an empire that stretched from the British Isles to the deserts of Africa. One gesture of his bony hand, as Tacitus wrote, was enough to unleash the Roman aircraft carriers.

"(OF INNER UNREST)"

213 There is a pun—untranslatable as puns generally are—on "Unruh," which in German means both "unrest" and the mainspring of a watch. (M.H.)

"BERLIN ROUNDS"

233 Tauentzienstrasse), *"a broken bottleneck"*: A reference to the Kaiser-Wilhelm-Gedächtniskirche Memorial Church on Kurfürstendamm street, in its guise as a preserved ruin.

235 Anhalter Bahnhof), *"The Mongol hordes"*: Refers to the Nazi propaganda technique designed to terrify and to mobilize the populace against the Red Army.

241 Epilogue), *"Goya's colossus"*: A reference to Francisco Goya's painting "The Colossus" in the Prado in Madrid.

"IN FRONT OF AN OLD X-RAY"

257 *"the House of Charred Furniture"*: The so-called *"Casa del mobilio carbonizzato"* in Herculaneum.

"VITA BREVIS"

261 *"History was no use to me"*: See Friedrich Nietzsche's *On the Use and Abuse of History for Life*.

"EUROPE AFTER THE LAST RAINS"

275 *"The fantasy mosque"*: The premises of the former cigarette factory Yenize, near the Elbe river.

275 *"the big garden"*: The Dresden Municipal Park.
279 *"Hiroshima"*: According to secret plans, Dresden was among the original targets for the dropping of an atom bomb.

"BERLIN POSTHUMOUS"

291 *"endless moping"*: Advertising slogan of a Berlin funeral director in the 1920s.